Lori —

I pray this devotional blesses you & equips you to stand strong in the Lord!

I Love you

BATTLE CRY
THIRTY-DAY DEVOTIONAL

Discover the Life-Changing Power
of
Intentional Thinking

SHERRY ROSE & JENNIFER MORIN

Copyright © 2015 Sherry Rose & Jennifer Morin.

All rights reserved. No part of this book may be used or reproduced by any means, graphic, electronic, or mechanical, including photocopying, recording, taping or by any information storage retrieval system without the written permission of the author except in the case of brief quotations embodied in critical articles and reviews.

Scripture quotations marked (TLB) are taken from The Living Bible copyright © 1971. Used by permission of Tyndale House Publishers, Inc., Carol Stream, Illinois 60188. All rights reserved.

Scripture quotations from THE MESSAGE. Copyright © by Eugene H. Peterson 1993, 1994, 1995, 1996, 2000, 2001, 2002. Used by permission of Tyndale House Publishers, Inc.

The Holy Bible, English Standard Version® (ESV®) Copyright © 2001 by Crossway, a publishing ministry of Good News Publishers. All rights reserved. ESV Text Edition: 2011

Scripture quotations taken from the New American Standard Bible®, Copyright © 1960, 1962, 1963, 1968, 1971, 1972, 1973, 1975, 1977, 1995 by The Lockman Foundation. Used by permission." (www.Lockman.org)

Scripture quotations marked (NIV) are taken from the Holy Bible, New International Version®, NIV®. Copyright © 1973, 1978, 1984, 2011 by Biblica, Inc.™ Used by permission of Zondervan. All rights reserved worldwide. www.zondervan.com The "NIV" and "New International Version" are trademarks registered in the United States Patent and Trademark Office by Biblica, Inc.™

WestBow Press books may be ordered through booksellers or by contacting:

WestBow Press
A Division of Thomas Nelson & Zondervan
1663 Liberty Drive
Bloomington, IN 47403
www.westbowpress.com
1 (866) 928-1240

Because of the dynamic nature of the Internet, any web addresses or links contained in this book may have changed since publication and may no longer be valid. The views expressed in this work are solely those of the author and do not necessarily reflect the views of the publisher, and the publisher hereby disclaims any responsibility for them.

Any people depicted in stock imagery provided by Thinkstock are models, and such images are being used for illustrative purposes only.
Certain stock imagery © Thinkstock.

ISBN: 978-1-5127-2024-2 (sc)
ISBN: 978-1-5127-2023-5 (e)

Library of Congress Control Number: 2015918987

Print information available on the last page.

WestBow Press rev. date: 12/28/2015

Contents

Preface..ix
Acknowledgments..xv
Introduction..xvii

    Opening Prayer xxi
    Foundational Scriptures xxiii
    Day 1   What Is a Battle Cry? 1
    Day 2   Intentional Thinking........................4

Battle Cry for Faith 9
    Day 3   Prayer Life 11
    Day 4   Peace of God 15
    Day 5   Dwell on Truth 19
    Day 6   Your Faithful Father......................27
    Day 7   Choose to Trust 30
    Day 8   Those Tricky Feelings...................33
    Day 9   Stand Up, Daughter!.....................41
    Day 10 A New Confidence 45
    Day 11 Be Brave 49

Battle Cry for Forgiveness 55
    Day 12 Embrace the Power 57
    Day 13 Stay Fixed 61
    Day 14 Overcomer 64
    Day 15 No Condemnation 71

Day 16	His Generous Love	74
Day 17	Mercy Every Day	77
Day 18	I Forgive	83
Day 19	I Release	87
Day 20	Free to Heal	91

Battle Cry for Obedience 97
Day 21	An Obedient Life	99
Day 22	A Grateful Heart	103
Day 23	Propelled by Love	106
Day 24	Sanctification	113
Day 25	Holy Spirit's Role	116
Day 26	Your Role	120
Day 27	The Choice to Surrender	127
Day 28	A Holy Pursuit	131
Day 29	The Garment of Humility	135
Day 30	The Final Day: Warrior On!	140

About the Authors 151

Preface

This devotional was birthed out of the momentum from a women's conference in August 2014. Battle Cry 2014 (a Beyond the Well Conference, www.beyondthewellconference.com) focused on learning to speak truth and stand on three pivotal Christian principles: faith, forgiveness, and obedience. As the conference ended, each woman wrote her own personal battle cry on a card. (The stack of those cards sits on my desk as a reminder of God's grace and goodness!) In looking at the heart cries represented on these cards, I began to see similarities in the needs, desires, and struggles of these powerful and amazing women. In addition, we offered a training series to further expand the principles and reach more women; their battle cries joined the stack as well.

At the end of 2014, the Lord began to prick my heart with the idea of writing this devotional. Little did I know that my life was about to be impacted by those four little words no woman ever wants to hear: "You have breast cancer." In January 2015 I received the diagnosis, and in February I underwent a double mastectomy and reconstructive surgery. Four weeks later, I led the last Battle Cry training series meeting! They say you can tell the strength of a woman by what it takes to stop her. I am an overcomer. My personal battle cry is "I trust my faithful Father, no matter what I see or feel!" This has been my heart's cry for more than twenty years and was birthed out of a broken heart of infertility. During my life, the Lord has taught me the power of intentional thinking from a place of scriptural understanding. I tell you these things so you know that I practice what Jennifer and I preach here—and from personal experience I can assure you that Jennifer practices it too. It's all to God's glory!

This is what I know of life. Life is a collection of moments that result in a treasure of memories and lessons learned. These moments are found in relationships, circumstances, and events. Some of those moments uplift us, and others shake us to our core. In one moment we may embrace a great victory, only to see it be followed by utter defeat. We have so much to look forward to in life, with its cherished memories and fulfilled dreams. But as anyone who's been alive five minutes can attest, life is also unpredictable, with uncertainties around every corner. Common to all these moments is an influential element that determines how the moments will shape us. This single element determines in great measure how we will walk into tomorrow having faced those moments. It is the belief behind our self-talk.

In our Christian experience, one of the most important beliefs to grasp is that *God is good*! We say to each other "God is good!" and receive the response "All the time!" But do we believe it—really believe it? Whether you've walked with God for thirty years or thirty minutes, His love and goodness already overcame you when you said yes to Jesus and the power of the cross. God already has a track record in your life! If your own testimony isn't enough to convince you of His goodness, would the Bible be enough? Have you ever read God's Word to seek out his goodness? Try it! Start with Psalm 145.

We are instructed in Scripture to "destroy arguments and every lofty opinion raised against the knowledge of God, and take every thought captive to obey Christ." (2 Corinthians 10:5 ESV). So, what is your self-talk saying about your belief in God's goodness? Is it lining up with Scripture? And what if the words you speak into your life were based on the honest belief that *God is good*? What might your self-talk sound like then? Wow! Would trusting Him be easier if you were fully convinced that He is always good? Could you speak life to yourself during a struggle, while embracing your identity as His daughter? How about forgiveness, the ultimate expression of God's goodness and love for you: Could you find yourself forgiving others because He forgave you? Surely it would be easier to live a life of obedience knowing that God is good and will always lead you in His ways, even if they don't make sense to you.

My heart persists with a desire to see God's daughters overcome. As I write this, I am still pressing through my healing process. God blessed me richly with the support and loving friendship of my coauthor, Jennifer Morin, who brings a rich history of walking with God through difficulty, disappointment, and heartbreak. She too is an overcomer! I didn't know what the Lord had in store when He asked me to write this devotional. But you can know it comes from the personal understanding that women need encouragement to become equipped to overcome.

Our devotional is a little different than most. Its purpose is not to pour truth into you. *Its purpose is to teach you how to pour truth into yourself.* Knowing how to confidently speak and believe the truths in the Scriptures for your life will empower you to walk in victory. Yes! You can have victory in all of life's moments, be they happy or distressing. From your time in the *Battle Cry* devotional, you will learn nine battle cries centered on three topics that are crucial to healthy Christian living: faith, forgiveness, and obedience. Each battle cry is designed to speak truth into your mind, encourage your heart, solidify your identity, and ultimately enrich your relationship with Jesus Christ. You will read a lot in the upcoming pages about identity, surrender, aligning with the cross, choosing to partner with the perspective of God's kingdom, and the power of words. *As you say the battle cry for each day, know that you are releasing the power of heaven over your life and perspective.*

When you're finished, we will encourage you to create your own custom battle cry or several of them if you wish. Your words, when based on Scripture, have the transformative power to fill your mind with the truth, correct the troubles of your heart, and overcome the Enemy's lies. *Satan and the ideas of this world cannot control your mind unless you submit it to them.* However, a mind submitted to God will find freedom. We pray that you will be both edified and refreshed over the next thirty days. Prepare to grow!

Warrior on!
Sherry Rose

Acknowledgments

From Sherry Rose

To my beautiful son and daughters—may your hearts forever be filled and transformed by the love and mercy of Jesus as you walk in the plans He has for each of you!

Thank you, Lord Jesus, for the privilege of pouring my heart and thoughts into the lives of readers, your daughters! Thank you for the trials in my life that taught me, stretched me, tested me, and created my heart to persevere in truth.

Thank you to my amazing husband, Kent, for always encouraging and supporting the ministry efforts God lays on my heart! Thank you for being a strong and dependable priest in our home. You bless me every day! You truly are my number two! I love you!

Thank you, Jennifer (also known as Comma Queen), for partnering with me and pouring your beautiful heart and energy into this project! I am blessed beyond measure by our first effort ministering as writers. I look forward to what Jesus has in store for us!

Thanks so much to our families and friends for your encouragement and input while reading this devotional as we were creating it! Your heart for us and God's kingdom shines brightly!

From Jennifer Morin

I want to first thank God, my Creator and Healer! Thank you, Lord, for saving me and gifting me with the ability to communicate the Word with such practical application. I love you forever, Jesus!

Thank you, David Morin. I am grateful for the gift God gave me in you. Thank you for completely supporting this project in every way possible.

Sherry, thank you! I am honored that you invited me to participate in the creation of this devotional. I pray God blesses your ministry a hundredfold for the pure heart you have to advance His kingdom.

I also thank Joyce Lee for proofreading and streamlining our writing. And thank you, Joan Lund, for reading our rough draft and affirming our message.

I dedicate this project to my two sons. I pray this is a testimony of what God can do with a willing and obedient heart. Just as God has great plans for me, so does He have great plans for you both! God has equipped and chosen you for a specific purpose here on earth. Chase after the dreams God gives you!

Introduction

Dear Daughter of the King,

Are you prepared for your mind-set to change? Your prayer life to evolve? Your sense of God's presence to intensify? Your faith and obedience to reach heights never before achieved? We hope so!

If you commit yourself to this devotional journey over the next thirty days, God will speak to you in ways you'd never expect. Our prayer is that your mind, heart, and spirit will become so saturated with biblical truth that life change will be inevitable. There will be no way around it. We pray that you, grounded and energized by His Word, will stand strong in the truth and develop unwavering faith amid adversity. We pray your intimacy with God will increase so much that you'll face life with triumphant confidence. We encourage you to share the cries of your heart, your struggles, woes, and even praises with God—your Father! It is "with God" that all things are made possible (Matthew 19:26).

- "With God" you will cultivate great faith.
- "With God" forgiveness becomes your natural response to those who hurt you.

- "With God" you develop the self-control to obey His Word and the Spirit's leading.

Our hope is that this devotional will cause you to reflect on God and the truth of His Word on a daily basis. If you will partner with the idea of *intentional thinking* as we describe in this devotional, your perspective will change. When you read, pray, meditate, and, yes, abide in His Word and the confirmation of the Holy Spirit, life is different. Sherry and I have both experienced great transformations by being open, transparent, and intimate with God on a daily basis. Abiding in the Lord keeps us fighting the good fight, running the race, and staying on the narrow path. We warrior on! And so can you.

We pray your relationship with God is fortified and your warrior spirit is ignited by this devotional. When you are convinced of biblical truths, you can confidently face your future despite any obstacles, struggles, and unfavorable circumstances. God empowers you to claim your victories! We strongly believe it is only through a deep, intimate friendship with God that you gain the faith necessary to live the obedient lifestyle Jesus calls you to live.

Over the next few weeks, you will learn nine battle cries intended to empower you to develop the boldness and courage necessary to fulfill God's calling on your life. Each day we pose questions in a section named

"Intentional Thinking" to help you practically apply the principles of that day's entry. The "Prayer" section provides a prayer to get you started. Please take the time to pray into each topic as you feel led. We've also provided verses in the "For Further Study" section so you can dig a little deeper into the Word of God. Every third day you will have an opportunity to respond to a few questions in a section named "Your Turn." We have posed these questions with the pure intention to get your mind and spirit engaged in the principles discussed in the preceding days. We want you to experience freedom and victory, and these come by reflecting with full transparency with God. The "Your Turn" section is a place where you can be raw with God and gain ground in your destiny. Please see this devotional as a tool in your spiritual arsenal. This has the capacity to ignite your faith as well as your ability to forgive people and obey the Lord.

We serve a good God and loving Father! We serve a gracious Savior—our great King—and a powerful Holy Spirit! You are victorious because the Lord is victorious in you! So with that, let's get started.

Warrior on!
Jennifer Morin

Opening Prayer

*Our Prayer for You, Daughter
of the Most High King!*

Based on Ephesians 3:14–20; Colossians 1:9–12; and Romans 12:1–2

Heavenly Father,

We bend our knees before You, Father, from whom every family in heaven and on earth derives its name, that You would grant to your daughter, according to the riches of Your glory, strength with power through Your Spirit in her inner being. May Christ dwell in her heart through faith; *and* may she, being rooted and grounded in love, be able to comprehend with all the saints the breadth and length and height and depth of Your love for her. May she know the love of Christ, which surpasses knowledge, and be filled up to all the fullness of You, God.

Because of her faith in You and her identity as Your cherished Holy Spirit–filled daughter, we pray Your blessing will not cease so she may be filled with the knowledge of Your will in all spiritual wisdom and understanding, so that she will walk in a manner worthy of You, Lord, pleasing You in all respects, bearing fruit in every good work and increasing in the knowledge of You; strengthened with all power, according to Your glorious might, for the attaining of all steadfastness and patience; joyously giving thanks to You, Father, who has qualified her to share in the inheritance of the saints in Your light.

Therefore, Lord, urge her, in view of Your mercy, to offer her body and soul as a living sacrifice, holy and pleasing to You, God, for this is her true and proper worship. Encourage her to not conform to the pattern of this world *but be transformed by the renewing of her mind*. Then she will be able to test and approve what Your will is—Your good, pleasing, and perfect will for her life!

We bless You, Lord! For You are able to do great things with our lives—indeed, providing far more abundance than we can ask for or imagine, according to Your power that works within us! May our lives reflect Your love, glory, and power! May we honor You in all we do and walk in the favor of Your kingdom and our calling! In the mighty name of Jesus we pray! Amen.

Foundational Scriptures

The Battle Cry

> The LORD will march out like a champion, like a warrior he will stir up his zeal; with a shout he will raise the battle cry and will triumph over his enemies. (Isaiah 42:13)

The Promise of Jesus

> I have told you these things, so that in me you may have peace. In this world you will have trouble. But take heart! I have overcome the world. (John 16:33)

God Is Good, Faithful, and Trustworthy

The Lord is gracious and compassionate; slow to anger and rich in love.

The Lord is good to all; he has compassion on all he has made.

All your works praise you, Lord; your faithful people extol you.

They tell of the glory of your kingdom and speak of your might so that all people may know of your mighty acts and the glorious splendor of your kingdom.

Your kingdom is an everlasting kingdom, and your dominion endures through all generations.

The Lord is trustworthy in all he promises and faithful in all he does.

The Lord upholds all who fall and lifts up all who are bowed down.

The eyes of all look to you, and you give them their food at the proper time.

You open your hand and satisfy the desires of every living thing.

The LORD is righteous in all his ways and
faithful in all he does.
The LORD is near to all who call on him, to all
who call on him in truth.
He fulfills the desires of those who fear him;
he hears their cry and saves them.
The LORD watches over all who love him, but
all the wicked he will destroy.
My mouth will speak in praise of the LORD.
Let every creature praise his holy name for ever
and ever. (Psalm 145:8–21)

Day 1

What Is a Battle Cry?

> The LORD will march out like a champion, like a warrior he will stir his zeal; with a shout he will raise the battle cry and triumph over his enemies.
> —Isaiah 42:13

Do we truly understand the mind-changing and heart-strengthening power of words—particularly our own words? Words really are our first line of defense as we overcome.

Isaiah 42:13 tells us that God does two things as He charges into battle. First, He stirs Himself up! In other words, He prepares and engages His heart into action. Then He raises the battle cry with a shout! For us, raising a battle cry requires embracing the truth, deciding what we will tell ourselves, and taking action based on that truth.

What does it mean to shout a battle cry? And is making a proclamation, even a loud one, enough? A battle cry is an announcement built on truth and is designed to inspire us into both greater belief and action. Our actions are the evidence of our true beliefs. Isaiah goes on to say that God triumphs. And He did! Jesus triumphed over our sins and our sinful nature on the cross. He triumphed again when He arose out of the grave, breaking the curse of death. Do you believe that triumph will enter your life if you submit to the love of Jesus, the truth of His Word, and the confirmation of the Holy Spirit? We hope so!

We are encouraged in Scripture to "seek first the kingdom of God and His righteousness" (Matthew 6:33 NASB). Every day, we are surrounded by an assortment of influences bombarding us with negativity. We are assaulted by Satan from all sides with lies, partial truths, and distorted, unscriptural points of view. We also need to beware the people, situations, and circumstances that confound and confuse us. But the most poisonous source of emotional and spiritual death comes from inside our own thinking! We must overcome our minds. We do this by seeking the truths of the Scripture, believing those truths, and shouting our battle cry!

This is what Scripture says: "For everyone who has been born of God overcomes the world. And this is the victory that has overcome the world—our faith" (1 John 5:4). So now you get to choose. Are you going to align yourself with the height of truth or with a lower ideal? Are you going to speak life or death into your heart, your mind, your relationships, and your situations—indeed, into your very existence?

Day 1

Be encouraged! God would not command us to overcome if it weren't possible. In John 16:33 Jesus tells us, "I have told you these things, so that in me you may have peace. In this world you will have trouble. But take heart! I have overcome the world." It is through Jesus that we have the power to overcome! It is His desire that we would be uplifted in our minds with the truth of the Scripture and through the power of the Holy Spirit. Today you begin a journey to transform your thinking into that of a warrior! God is the greatest warrior, and you are His child. Let your warrior spirit arise!

Intentional Thinking: Based on these truths, how would developing your own battle cry help you overcome a current challenge in your life? How would partnering with God affect your thoughts and actions today?

Prayer: Thank You, Lord Jesus! You have defeated all evil and all death! You are the greatest warrior and the creator and inspiration of all truth. Today I submit my mind into Your strong and tender hands for sharpening. I submit my heart to You for comfort and counsel. I acknowledge my great need for You and will listen for Your voice today as I warrior on! In Jesus's name, amen.

For Further Study: Proverbs 18:20–21; 1 Corinthians 15:55–57; Romans 12:1–2.

Day 2

Intentional Thinking

To be made new in the attitude of your minds.
—Ephesians 4:23

Some of the sagest advice ever given is this: "Be very careful what you tell yourself about how you feel." You may not be able to choose how you feel in a situation, especially if there are wounds from the past in your heart. However, you are able to choose what you will think about the situation and your feelings. You get to decide the attitude or position you will take in response to those feelings. You *can* think intentionally.

The first key to intentional thinking is to understand that emotions aren't necessarily right or wrong and that they are terrible assessors of the situation at hand. Paul advises in Ephesians to choose to think with a new mind.

> That, however, is not the way of life you learned when you heard about Christ and were taught in

> him in accordance with the truth that is in Jesus. You were taught, with regard to your former way of life, to put off your old self, which is being corrupted by its deceitful desires; to be made new in the attitude of your minds; and to put on the new self, created to be like God in true righteousness and holiness. (Ephesians 4:20–24)

The second key to intentional thinking is to *speak* the truth, which comes from *knowing* the truth. Having meditated on the Scriptures to transform your mind, you can lean on the counsel of the Word and the Holy Spirit before you respond. The power to choose what you will think is available to you. But you have to know the truth to speak the truth. Your mind—that part of you that exists in the four inches between your temples—is the most powerful and dangerous part of who you are! We all wrestle with our thoughts every day. King David wrote in Psalm 13:2, "How long must I wrestle with my thoughts?" His son Solomon answered this question for us in Proverbs 4:7: "The beginning of wisdom is this: Get wisdom. Though it cost all you have, get understanding." This is where you start; open your Bible to get the wisdom.

The third key to intentional thinking is to "put on the new self" (Ephesians 4:24). This requires action. It takes more than just knowing you *can* think differently; it is *deciding to* think differently. We are empowered by 2 Corinthians 10:5 (NASB), which tells us to "take every thought captive to the obedience of Christ." Through the power of the Holy Spirit, intentional thinking will overcome self-will, emotions, pride, vain imaginations, and the like. This requires a change of mind that only comes from actively deciding to lay down your thinking and replace it with God's thinking. This is what we mean when we refer to "having a kingdom perspective."

For the next twenty-eight days, you will be given the opportunity to speak truth into your life. If you embrace your identity and the intentions of the nine battle cries we are going to present, you will be stronger and more fortified. If you put these truths to work in your life, your mind will be clearer and your warrior heart can ignite!

Some of the topics will be a reminder to you of the foundational truths we embrace and engage in as Christians. Others will be presented in a manner to deepen your understanding and challenge you to embrace a kingdom perspective in a fresh way. Each day we hope to build your faith, encourage your heart, sharpen your thinking, and inspire a deeper connection with the Holy Spirit, thus equipping you to be an overcomer. It is in knowing and believing God's Word that you have the authority to speak and respond out of truth—to shout your battle cry!

Intentional Thinking: What are you telling yourself about how you feel? And what does God have to say about that? Put this practice to work in your life now. Soon enough, an opportunity will present itself and you will get to choose. Will you respond out of emotion or out of right, intentional thinking?

Prayer: Thank You, Lord, that Your Holy Spirit is willing and ready to help me take my thoughts captive. Thank You, Lord, that You make a way for me to be made new, with a new mind in Christ. Today I ask You for the power to take action, speak truth over my life and circumstances, and keep Your kingdom perspective. In Jesus's name, amen.

For Further Study: Psalm 13:2; Proverbs 4:4–7; Isaiah 55:6–8; Luke 5:22; 9:23.

Battle Cry for

Faith

Days 3–5

My life of prayer produces peace and right thinking!

Day 3

Prayer Life

Battle Cry: *My life of prayer produces peace and right thinking!*

> Be anxious for nothing, but in everything by prayer and supplication with thanksgiving let your requests be made known to God. And the peace of God, which surpasses all comprehension, will guard your hearts and your minds in Christ Jesus.
> —Philippians 4:6–7 (NASB)

Prayer is your lifeline to the Lord. He is forever available for you to run to and communicate with. If you trust Him as the Savior of your soul, you can trust Him with your future, your emotions, and your concerns. Philippians 4:6–7 speaks to this very practice of surrendering your needs to God and turning them into conversations with Him.

Faith

That passage from Philippians is commonly quoted as a solution to real-life problems. Yet hearing the verse and saying the verse is *not* what quiets anxious thoughts. *Doing* what the verse says is how we experience the promised peace of God. As James 1:22 exhorts us, let's be doers of the Word, not just hearers!

Today let's look in Philippians 4 at verse 6: "But in everything by prayer and supplication with thanksgiving let your requests be made known to God." Stop and envision how *prayer, supplication,* and *thanksgiving* used together keep you anchored in God. These three components of a prayer life strengthen your faith as you hope, contend, and persevere.

Prayer is addressing your needs with God. It is imperative as a Christian—as a disciple of Christ—that you have a healthy prayer connection with God. This is your communication line to the Almighty over your *entire life*. Your prayer life is vital to having an intimate relationship with your Lord, Jesus Christ.

Supplication goes a step beyond the simplicity of a prayer. Supplication is a humble, deeply sincere request, an intense and tenacious asking—asking to the point of begging. Supplicating is staying determined to remain fixed on God until He answers; it is continually requesting until an answer comes.

Thanksgiving is the grateful acknowledgment of divine favors that accompanies your requests. Today's

Day 3

verse, then, implies that your faith is fully engaged and God is already moving into action because of your prayers and supplications. Do you believe this is true? Giving thanks to God for what He is doing in advance demonstrates your assurance that He is faithfully at work in your life's circumstances. Always remember: thanksgiving is key to dealing with anxious thoughts.

Daily, we face people and situations that flood our minds with anxious thoughts. Late bills, a diagnosis, an argument with a loved one, a car accident, a sick friend, or even death are all possible peace stealers. Trials and tribulations will come, but the Lord has provided us a method of finding and keeping peace in the midst of the chaos. What would it look like if you immediately addressed God with your deep, sincere requests, followed by a thank-you? Life would be different because of the peace that would dwell abundantly in your heart and mind. It is time to respond to situations and relationships through prayer, supplication, and thanksgiving. Start today!

Intentional Thinking: Is your life of prayer producing peace and right thinking? Based on the truths discussed today, will you decide to instantly stop your anxious thoughts so as to pray and lift up all requests and needs surrounding the situation to God? How will prayer affect your thinking and response to life today?

Prayer: Thank You, Lord Jesus, for Your sovereignty in my life. I acknowledge that Your love and protection will intervene in my life today. Empower me to trust You with circumstances out of my control. I choose to stop my anxious thoughts and cast all my cares on You. Keep me mindful of Your truth and sensitive to the Holy Spirit. In Jesus's name, amen.

For Further Study: Jeremiah 29:12–13; 33:3; Matthew 7:7; Luke 18:3–5; Hebrews 11:6; 1 John 5:14–15.

Day 4

Peace of God

Battle Cry: *My life of prayer produces peace and right thinking!*

> Be anxious for nothing, but in everything by prayer and supplication with thanksgiving let your requests be made known to God. And the peace of God, which surpasses all comprehension, will guard your hearts and your minds in Christ Jesus …
> —Philippians 4:6–7 (NASB)

Aren't we all searching for peace in this life? We can't find it on television, on the Internet, in relationships, or in the marketplace. We look to take our mind off things with a sitcom, but the commercials flood us with discontentment and the news update reminds us of the war zones around the world. The Internet momentarily diverts us with updates and posts, but those often cause insecurities or disappointments. Life becomes stressful, and too often we rely too much on others for comfort

Faith

and distraction. Where can we escape from the angst and find peace?

What does the peace of God look like? The passage from Philippians says that this peace "surpasses all comprehension" and that it "guards our hearts and minds in Christ Jesus." Consider Philippians 4:7 from the Living Bible: "If you do this, you will experience God's peace, which is far more wonderful than the human mind can understand. His peace will keep your thoughts and your hearts quiet and at rest as you trust in Christ Jesus."

This verse illustrates a spiritual principle of giving to God and receiving from God—an exchange. Do you realize there is so much peace you can access? The peace of Jesus, the Prince of Peace, is accessible to you. His peace is surpassing: exceeding, outdoing, and transcending all that our minds can fathom, understand, or grasp intellectually. His peace surpasses concerns, threats, and anxieties. Have you experienced this peace yet? Have you clung to the cloak of Jesus with faith, praying until you have reached His presence that soothes your soul? This verse is a promise that you can have and experience God's abounding peace. It belongs to you!

Beware of the counterfeits of the Enemy! An absence of strife or conflict is not the transcending peace of God. The Lord's peace is a powerful, comforting force in the depths of your soul. Yesterday, we established that this peace from God begins from a life of prayer, supplication, and thanksgiving (Philippians 4:6–7). Additionally, the Message Bible reminds us of the importance of worship in our pursuit of peace in verse 6: " ... Let petitions and *praises* shape your worries into prayers, letting God know your concerns ..." Understanding these foundational principles equips you to find the peace of God for which you've been searching so long.

Why is it so important for a believer to have this peace? God's peace guards our hearts and minds from making quick, panicked decisions out of dread or terror. Panic is an antonym to peace. God's peace provides protection over our minds and hearts. Finding His peace prevents emotions from running our lives. We need His peace to govern all our responses to what comes our way. Daughter, the Holy Spirit is willing and ready to overwhelm you with peace. Embrace it!

Intentional Thinking: Your prayer life produces peace and right thinking. How will this battle cry and the Scriptures from today's reading affect your search for God and His peace? Where do you need this peace that belongs to you today? And what will you do to find it?

Faith

Prayer: Thank You, Lord, that Your peace shields my mind from fear. Your peace gives me strength in chaos and crisis. Holy Spirit, I call on You to anoint me with power for prayer and worship. God, I exalt You above my sufferings and set You on high as Lord over all! In Jesus's name, amen.

For Further Study: Proverbs 3:5–6; Isaiah 9:6; Luke 7:50; John 14:27; 16:33; Ephesians 3:20.

Day 5

Dwell on Truth

Battle Cry: *My life of prayer produces peace and right thinking!*

> Finally, brethren, whatever is true, whatever is honorable, whatever is right, whatever is pure, whatever is lovely, whatever is of good repute, if there is any excellence and if anything worthy of praise, dwell on these things.
> —Philippians 4:8 (NASB)

Our goal is a focused thought life that glorifies God and produces fruit in our lives. As children of God, let's acquire a kingdom perspective. When our thoughts line up with God's Word, we will find that we walk with greater confidence and discernment. If we let God's view govern our thoughts, we find ourselves with right thinking. To keep our kingdom perspective, we must filter our thoughts through God's Word and take every thought captive to the obedience of Christ (2 Corinthians 10:5).

Faith

The last couple of days, we focused on the power of prayer over our thoughts and how a persistent prayer life ushers in God's peace. Let's learn to dwell in this peace daily. We have established that our thoughts are potent. Our verse for today clearly states what we are to allow our minds to dwell on. Here is further explanation to define what we should accept and agree with in our minds.

- **True:** *truth lines up with God's Word*
- **Honorable:** *reverent and respectful*
- **Right:** *innocent, faultless, approved by God*
- **Pure:** *chaste and modest*
- **Lovely:** *acceptable, pleasing*
- **Of good repute:** *life-giving words, praiseworthy success*
- **Excellent:** *morally good*
- **Worthy of praise:** *admirable*

What if we were to use these words as a report card on our thought life? Consider your thoughts today, yesterday, last week. When you consider this list of what one should dwell on, do you find that your thoughts lining up? Take a minute now to underline the items you need to work on right away. Where the mind goes, the mouth follows. Imagine how encouraged your family and coworkers would be if the words of your mouth reflected these meditations in your heart. Proverbs 16:23–24 (NASB) says, "The heart of the wise instructs his mouth and adds persuasiveness to his lips. Pleasant words are a honeycomb, sweet to the soul and healing to the bones."

Day 5

Are you catching the vision? Prayer to God about our woes and needs, partnered with praises, makes us aware of His presence. Remember: God inhabits the praises of His people (Psalm 22:3). A quiet time of communion with God allows us to receive His view of our situations, and it gives Him a chance to confirm and affirm to us that He is with us that moment. In His presence is where we find His peace that completely exceeds our understanding. In His presence is where we are empowered to trust Him with our circumstances. It is also here that we cultivate the soil of our hearts for the harvest of godly speech. The Word of God calls us to be proactive and control our thought lives and emotions. We must dwell on things that are pure, respectful, virtuous, and approved by God to keep our thinking focused on and aligned with a heavenly perspective.

Intentional Thinking: Has the battle cry "My life of prayer produces peace and right thinking!" affected your thoughts and prayers this week? Will you be intentional with dwelling on the truth? Do you expect to find more peace because of your prayers?

Prayer: Thank You, Lord, that You truly are a prayer away. Thank You for the power to overcome through prayer, petitions, and thanksgiving in my life. I ask that You keep me at a place of dependency on You so

Faith

that I can be strong and triumphant in life. Lord, I continually thank You for all You have shown me and confirmed in Your Word. You are awesome, God. In Jesus's name, amen.

For Further Study: Joshua 1:8; Psalm 27:4; 49:3; 63:6; 145:5; Romans 12:1–2.

Your Turn

Let's personalize this verse and battle cry according to your life. What are some unhealthy thoughts you have been dwelling on lately? Can you trace back to the source of those thoughts? What thoughts and actions have led you to experience God's peace in the past? In the space here describe what you will choose to think about as you set your mind on the course to find God's peace.

Battle Cry for

Faith

Days 6–8

I trust my faithful God no matter what I see or feel!

Day 6

Your Faithful Father

Battle Cry: *I trust my faithful God no matter what I see or feel!*

> If we are faithless, He remains faithful, For He cannot deny Himself.
> —2 Timothy 2:13 (NASB)

As you pursue a triumphant victory for this life, you must keep your warrior mind-set and overcoming spirit engaged daily. In order to walk in confidence despite circumstances, we must resolve to this foundational belief: God is faithful.

God's character and nature is faithfulness. Faithfulness is truth. When we think of faithfulness, we think of being true to one's word and promise, continually stable, reliable, and steady in allegiance and affection. Faithfulness is constant trustworthiness and loyalty. God is all of these things: stable, steady in His affection and love for you, trustworthy, and loyal. Because God cannot deny Himself, He is reliable and true to His Word, His promises. Are you believing this? Do you believe is faithful? God is faithful. Say it with me: "God *is* faithful!"

In order for you to carry on from here, you must believe in your core that God truly loves you, He is good, and He is faithful. Yes, God loves you! You must believe this truth in order to trust Him, His Word, and His Spirit. This truth must rule your heart, regardless what you see or feel.

Let's stop here. Is there is a situation (what you see) or a hurt or concern (what you feel) in your life preventing you from believing that God is faithful and He loves you? If not, good! Thank Him for His goodness to you. If so, ask God to reveal the lie behind the emotions that leads you to doubt Him. Ask Him to reveal His goodness in the situation that has you doubting His faithfulness. And thank Him for His goodness and faithfulness to you. You have to choose to believe He is good and faithful. If you use own life experiences to determine His faithfulness and goodness, you are judging Him using the wrong lens. He is good and faithful because He says He is. You can believe Him!

Consider the triune God's acts of love and faithfulness. We see God the Father is faithful, for He sent His Son to the cross. We see God the Son is faithful, for He endured death on the cross for our sins and rose again to redeem us. And we see God the Spirit is faithful, for He continually guides, counsels, and leads us through our lives with conviction and power.

Life can jade us. People will disappoint us, and our vision of who God really is can become skewed. We must refuse to allow our letdowns from life block our view of a completely trustworthy and loving God. Ask God to renew your mind and give you a fresh vision of who He really is so that the truth of God's faithfulness rules your heart and mind. He will renew your mind and clear your path—just keep your eyes open for Him!

Intentional Thinking: We are called to trust our faithful God no matter what we see or feel. Based on today's Scripture, how will you direct your thinking with this statement? How will these truths affect your behavior today?

Prayer: Lord, thank You for the power of the Holy Spirit, who enables me to do all that You are calling me to. I praise You, Lord, for Your faithfulness and complete sovereignty over my life. Today I choose to acknowledge You in all my ways and find Your love and presence in my life. You are good and faithful. In Jesus's name, amen.

For Further Study: Genesis 12:10–13:4; Deuteronomy 7:9; Proverbs 3:5–6; Hebrews 6:16–18.

Day 7

Choose to Trust

Battle Cry: *I trust my faithful God no matter what I see or feel!*

> And without faith it is impossible to please Him, for he who comes to God must believe that He is and that He is a rewarder of those who seek Him.
> —Hebrews 11:6 (NASB)

Which came first: God's faithfulness or our faith and trust in Him? The initial four words in the Bible at Genesis 1:1 say, "In the beginning God ..." We established yesterday that God is faithful; this is His perpetuating, unchanging, steady character. God cannot deny Himself. He is faithfulness in its entirety.

We are called to believe in this faithful God, but how do we establish this as our personal reality? How do we experience God's faithfulness? Choose to engage with Him. Communicate with Him. Obediently follow

Him. Our role in our relationship with God cannot be passive—we must take initiative and be proactive in it. Consider this proactive verse:

> Ask, and it will be given to you; seek and you will find; knock, and it will be opened to you. For everyone who asks receives, and he who seeks finds, and to him who knocks it will be opened ... how much more will your Father who is in heaven give what is good to those who ask Him! (Matthew 7:7–8, 11 NASB)

God in His faithfulness is always there for us, yet we must engage with Him, open our hearts and our eyes to Him to experience Him. It is through our asking, seeking, and obeying of God that we experience Him and His trustworthy presence firsthand.

> Then you will call upon Me and come and pray to Me, and I will listen to you. You will seek Me and find Me when you search for Me with all your heart. (Jeremiah 29:12–13 NASB)

That is a verse that you can stand on! There is no reason to believe that God is not listening to your sincere requests. He is attentive to His children. He is your good and faithful Father. His eyes are searching the face of the earth looking for those whose hearts are completely His (2 Chronicles 16:9). When you seek Him, not only will you find Him, but also He will speak with you.

> Call to Me and I will answer you, and I will tell you great and mighty things, which you do not know. (Jeremiah 33:3 NASB)

But how do you trust God? Take Him at His word. Recall what He has already done for you. Surrender the people, trials, and circumstances that have left you feeling defeated as you call out to God! Get ahold of the Spirit of God for His wisdom and insight as you pursue a healthy kingdom perspective. It is through seeking, asking, and searching for God's answers and help that you gain the experiential knowledge to ignite your faith and build your trust. When you search for Him, believe you will find Him. Stay in constant pursuit of Him!

Intentional Thinking: We choose to trust our faithful God no matter what we see or feel. Based on the Scriptures of today, choose this day whom you will trust. How will these truths affect your prayers, thoughts, and decisions today?

Prayer: I praise You, Lord, for faithful care of me. Just as Psalm 91:2 says, You alone are "my refuge and my fortress, my God in whom I trust." I surrender my thinking to Your Spirit and choose to trust and depend on You with all of my being. In Jesus's name, amen!

For Further Study: Psalm 91; Isaiah 49; Psalm 22:5; Romans 10:11.

Day 8

Those Tricky Feelings

Battle Cry: *I trust my faithful God no matter what I see or feel!*

The heart is deceitful above all things and beyond cure. Who can understand it?

"I the LORD search the heart and examine the mind, to reward each person according to their conduct, according to what their deeds deserve."
—Jeremiah 17:9–10

It is amazing to how one insult amongst ten compliments will set your whole day on a downward spiral. People, especially women, take their feelings very seriously and often rely too heavily on their influences when making decisions about themselves and life. As you remember from Day 2, we emphasized that emotions aren't necessarily right or wrong and that they are terrible assessors of the situation at hand. Feelings are an unreliable copilot! They are loud and sure footed in expressing themselves, and they can easily steer us off course if we let them. The Lord warns us of the trouble with the human heart, calling it "deceitful about all things and beyond cure!" God then says that He will examine the mind as it responds to the heart. This is why intentional thinking is so important. What do you want God to find as He examines your mind?

When looking at feelings, we often talk about negative emotions caused by wounds and disappointments, emotions such as anger, jealousy, vengefulness, shame, depression, anxiety, and guilt. However, there are an entirely different set of emotions that we must also keep in check! Positive emotions such as feelings of love, excitement, inspiration, amusement, and the like can get us in a ton of trouble too!

Our response to the world around us must be based on the Word and our relationship with God—nothing else. We must constantly be on the lookout for the kingdom perspective—not our emotional perspective, even when it's positive. You can be sure Satan is lurking to influence you to deviate from your healthy kingdom mind-set. We tend to think God has things going our way if we "feel" good in the situation. This is a tricky thing to consider! Here's why: Satan is happy to keep you happy! After all, which of us want to rock the boat in life and risk losing the warm-fuzzy feelings, the contentment, or the zeal associated with new

Day 8

opportunities or dreams unfolding? Undeniably, Satan is banking on our likelihood to make decisions based on our emotions, be they happy or sad!

Back on Day 2, we learned "Be very careful what you tell yourself about how you feel"! Here's a practical approach to what we're talking about. One of the biggest challenges we face is identifying how we feel and the source of that feeling. So many things from your life will contribute to and have a voice in your current situation. Ever notice that something small and seemingly inconsequential can stir up a big emotional response? If you aren't sure that is true, consider how you felt the last time someone cut you off in line at the supermarket. Feelings of anger and frustration, even indignation, surface because someone inconvenienced you by six minutes! You may be able to identify anger, but it's more likely hurt feelings that are speaking so loudly to your heart and mind. The only way to assess the truth is to go directly to the source of all truth, the Holy Spirit inside you! He may bring to mind the girl who bullied you in fourth grade by cutting in front of you in the lunch line every day. Or maybe your current feelings of frustration stem from your high school "bestie" dumping you for the new girl at school, which left you feeling devalued and invisible.

God wants to teach you to be an advocate for you own heart by knowing the Holy Spirit and speaking His truth. Here's what the Lord says about His love for you and loving yourself.

Faith

> Dear children, let us not love with words or speech but with actions and in truth. This is how we know that we belong to the truth and how we set our hearts at rest in His presence: If our hearts condemn us, we know that God is greater than our hearts, and he knows everything. (1 John 3:18–20)

Navigating emotions is tricky business. And according to today's Scripture, the Lord will reward you according to your behavior, which stems from your emotions. God is just as concerned about how you respond based on your emotions as He is about the emotions themselves. Let Proverbs 28:26 convince you: "A man is a fool to trust himself! But those who use God's wisdom are safe." Sometimes the emotional pain we experience from life comes from a deep place, and it can be triggered by seemingly insignificant events in unexpected ways.

God is in the emotional healing business. His healing is readily available for your emotions if you seek Him. Choose to submit your heart to the examination of the Father and receive His evaluation. In doing this you can live an emotionally healthy life. Let His assessment of what hurts or pleases you be the truth you stand on. You can trust your faithful Father, no matter what you see or feel.

Intentional Thinking: What are you telling yourself about what you see and how you feel? What do you want God to find as He examines your mind today? Think about the emotions you wrestle with. Ask the Lord to reveal the truth about them and to heal them. Choose to believe His truth for your life.

Prayer: Thank You, Father, for loving me and my emotional side. I submit my heart with its emotions, happy or sad, for Your loving review. Give me the strength I need to understand and respond in healthy ways to my emotions. Today, Lord, I seek Your truth. I will stop and listen for Your kindness and grace as I go through my day. In Jesus's name, amen.

For Further Study: Psalm 26:2; Jeremiah 11:20; 31:33; Romans 8:27; Philippians 4:7; 1 John 3:20.

Your Turn

Do you believe God is faithful? In what ways do you show God that you trust Him? What kind of words do you speak over yourself? Do your thoughts contradict the Word of God? Is your heart connecting with the truths of the Scriptures? What are some thoughts you had this week that interfered with your relationships with God or others? Will you surrender to the truth that God is faithful?

Battle Cry for

Faith

Days 9–11

I am the King's daughter; confidence and courage belong to me!

Day 9

Stand Up, Daughter!

Battle Cry: *I am the King's daughter; confidence and courage belong to me!*

> The Spirit himself testifies with our spirit that we are God's children.
> —Romans 8:16

As we continue our journey into a deeper faith in God, it is crucial that we truly grasp who we are. What does it mean to be the "King's daughter?" Take a look at this Scripture and consider your standing with God. It is on this promise that you can secure your heart to His!

> For those who are led by the Spirit of God are the children of God. The Spirit you received does not make you slaves, so that you live in fear again; rather, the Spirit you received brought about your adoption to sonship. And by him we cry, "Abba, Father." The Spirit himself testifies with our spirit that we are God's children. (Romans 8:14–16)

By your own testimony you know that you were once a sinner, but the Scriptures say that you are now made new: a brand new creation (2 Corinthians 5:17). This is great news! It means that the overwhelming power to walk with the authority and privilege of the King's daughter belongs to you! However, we don't embrace the brand new easily, nor do we know how to wield that power. We might ask ourselves, *How do I live as this new creation? What does it mean to be an heir? After all, I'm still me, and these are still my thoughts and emotions and story and family and circumstances. So how am I made new?* The *new* comes as you daily make the choice to allow the Holy Spirit to reign in your heart and transform your mind. The change comes when we honestly and lovingly assess ourselves to confront anything that stands against our true identity. We decide to say goodbye to what holds us captive as slaves: harsh self-assessment, our sin nature, other people, labels and distorted gender roles, alliances with ungodliness, and all sorts of other influences that we readily define ourselves by.

Just to be clear: what we are saying here is that you must stand in your new identity by overcoming all misunderstanding and wrong beliefs about yourself. We recognize that this is a tall order! Here's some good news: *The Lord is gracious and compassionate, slow to anger and rich in love* (Psalm 145:8). Let the Holy Spirit reveal any area in your life that comes against the truth of who you really are. Your life, when submitted to the

Day 9

Holy Spirit, will be transformed! It's kind of like being in Royalty School: you have to learn how to become this new creation, how to recognize who you really are, and how to walk in royal authority. Ask the Holy Spirit for godly teachers to encourage the growth and changes you want to see in your thinking, behavior, and life.

We have another piece of good news for you: You are not your sin! Joy in life comes from knowing your identity in Christ, which can never be stripped from you! You'll stumble and fall, but this doesn't make you less of an heir—you are still the daughter of the Most High God! Your commitment to remain submitted to the Holy Spirit will reveal your identity. As a daughter of the King you have access to this kingdom principle. The more you come into alignment with this truth, the less you stumble. Stand on that truth!

Intentional Thinking: Today's battle cry claims confidence and courage because of your identity as the King's daughter. When you have thoughts about yourself today, ask this question: *What would God say to me about who I am?*

Prayer: Thank You, Holy Spirit, for making me new! Thank You for assisting me every step of the way on my journey. Keep me alert to Your voice. Give me strength to recognize and release unhealthy thinking and behaviors to Your Lordship. I embrace Your truth. I claim my inheritance in Christ and walk confidently as an heir. I am the King's daughter! In Jesus's name, amen.

For Further Study: Galatians 4:7; 6:8–9; James 1:19; 2 Timothy 2:22.

Day 10

A New Confidence

Battle Cry: *I am the King's daughter; confidence and courage belong to me!*

> I remain confident of this: I will see the goodness of the Lord in the land of the living.
>
> Wait for the Lord; be strong and take heart and wait for the Lord.
>
> —Psalm 27:13–14

As women, we are natural problem-solvers. We have a new opportunity every day to exhibit how clever and ingenious our Father created us to be! For most of us, confidence, at least on some level, comes easy. We were designed to overcome and press on! This type of confidence is an easy snare for us to get caught up in with an "I can do this!" frame of mind. And yes, God created us with abilities and talents, creativity and ambition, and a strong survival instinct. All of these

Faith

traits are God-given and useful for problem-solving and communication. Consider this though: What if our highest confidence was placed *only* in God's goodness and power?

The confidence we will explore today comes from another place. It comes from a belief so bound to your soul that even the darkest storms can't strip it away. This confidence is that God knows your every need and concern; He is actively engaged on your behalf. Even in times of great shaking, confidence placed in God and His goodness will not be crushed! It says, "Since God already has this worked out, I will trust and follow Him." However, this isn't always easy when faced with a monstrous threat, an unending difficulty or joy robbing grief, but it's the only option! God knows the challenges of your life. He's got this!

> We are hard pressed on every side, but not crushed; perplexed, but not in despair; persecuted, but not abandoned; struck down, but not destroyed. (2 Corinthians 4:8–9)

So what do you do when life's difficulties overwhelm you, decisions you've made disappointment you, and closed doors discourage you? What do you do when you lack confidence? First, you give yourself a break! There is enough to beat you down in the world, you must be your own advocate! It is in these times that you intentionally think on the truth of who God is: He is good! He is faithful! He is trustworthy! Once your

Day 10

mind is set on the truth, get up, brush yourself off, and press on! God loves a tenacious heart! He doesn't say to be confident when we get things right. We are to be confident because we are His! Believe He is faithful and that in His goodness He has a plan for your life! (Romans 8:28)

Walking through life with confidence of who God is and who you are in Him, requires that you are able to identify the source of your struggles. The Holy Spirit, as your counselor and guide, will reveal things to you if you seek Him openly. Psalm 139:23–24 (NASB) demonstrates the prayer of a heart submitted to God's goodness: *"Search me, O God, and know my heart; Try me and know my anxious thoughts; And see if there be any hurtful way in me, And lead me in the everlasting way."* This list of questions will help you uncover the source of your trials.

- Did I take a misstep along the way? Is there an area of disobedience?
- Did Satan trip me up? Have I believed a lie or partnered with sin?
- Is my mind set on the truth? Do I know what the Word says about the situation?
- Is an emotion, like fear or shame, preventing me from believing in God's goodness?
- Am I allowing the Holy Spirit to calm my nerves, heal my heart, and love me?

Faith

Confidence belongs to you as a daughter of the King! Always remember that being confident has little to do with how you feel about yourself and everything to do with what you choose to believe about God. Step out today in the confidence of your trustworthy and mighty Father!

Intentional Thinking: Because you are the King's daughter, confidence and courage belong to you. Where in your life do these truths need to be applied? How does confidence in God change your perspective on your situations and relationships?

Prayer: Lord, thank You that I am not alone, ever! I praise You for Your power and goodness. Thank You that I have access to it too! I pray that I would be fully aware of Your presence today. Keep me steadfast in my confidence and strong in my courage. You truly are my source of power. Thank You Lord! In Jesus's name, amen.

For Further Study: James 1:2–6; Colossians 1:9–12; Philippians 3:8–12.

Day 11

Be Brave

Battle Cry: *I am the King's daughter; confidence and courage belong to me!*

> This is my command—be strong and courageous! Do not be afraid or discouraged. For the Lord your God is with you wherever you go.
> —Joshua 1:9

If you recall the journey of the Israelites, you know that Joshua was facing giants—literally! However, he knew that on the other side of the threat was the Promised Land. Yesterday, we talked about placing our confidence in God by choosing to trust in His ways and knowing that His love for us is without compromise or limit. Courage goes a step further. Courage responds to that confidence by stepping into the uncertain things of life. During these times we are called to remain in alignment with God and submitted. We are to remain

Faith

in a place of peace, even when things are uncertain, unfamiliar, or frightening. Every day we must be brave in the face of circumstances, change, and the unknown!

You may be asking, "But I'm afraid—so how do I respond courageously in the face of fear?" That is a reasonable question. Some things in life are really hard and frightening! A diagnosis, a job loss, an accident, and the like are all peace-threatening events. They require bravery on an entirely different level. However, sometimes the threat comes from less challenging situations like an unbearable coworker, a flat tire, or a disgruntled neighbor. Whatever the challenge, bravery is your only recourse.

There are two foundational truths of Christian living that will support you as you press on. The first is this: keep your eyes on God! Peter could only walk on the water (a physical impossibility) as long as his eyes were fixed on Jesus! (See Matthew 14:22–33.) The moment he looked at his circumstance, he sank. Even then, Jesus rescued him! Consider this prayer of Moses in Deuteronomy 3:24: "Sovereign LORD, you have begun to show to your servant your greatness and your strong hand. For what God is there in heaven or on earth who can do the deeds and mighty works you do?" Be aware that there is no force under heaven, neither your ability nor the world's promises, that can compare with the potential of God to see you through

Day 11

your challenges—and He loves you! Keep your eyes on Him alone!

The second truth to put to work in your life is this: the power of praise and positive words! Encourage yourself with songs of praise. Consider 1 Thessalonians 5:16–18, which says, "Rejoice always, pray continually, and give thanks in all circumstances; for this is God's will for you in Christ Jesus." Give yourself permission to talk to yourself—out loud: "God will not forsake me!"; "I am a chosen child of the Most High God!"; "I am an overcomer!" Use Scriptures like the following to encourage yourself with truth.

- **Psalm 103:8:** *The Lord is compassionate and gracious, slow to anger, abounding in love.*
- **Romans 8:31:** *What, then, shall we say in response to these things? If God is for us, who can be against us?*
- **Philippians 4:13:** *I can do all things through him who gives me strength.*

On Day 2 we talked about *intentional thinking*. In the same manner we must be intentional about the words we are speaking. Speak these truths even when you don't believe them. The Word's testimony of who you are and who God is stands high above yours. Choose to be courageous today! You know that God, who is in the midst of your challenges, provides a way through your obstacles.

Intentional Thinking: As a confident and courageous daughter of the King, which challenge will you face today? Based on these truths, will you press on to overcome obstacles in your life because of your renewed confidence in God?

Prayer: Thank you, Lord, that the victory is Yours! Calm my anxieties; fill my heart with peace; clear my mind; and give me the next step to take. You already have a way for my challenges to be overcome. Give me the spiritual eyes to see your hand at work. Increase my faith to carry on. I exalt You above all circumstances and walk in Your truth today. I am brave! In Jesus's name, amen.

For Further Study: Romans 8:37; Ephesians 6:10–11; Philippians 4:19; 2 Corinthians 9:8.

Your Turn

What does it mean to you to be the daughter of the King? Do you feel empowered today? Saturating your mind with these truths should shift your thinking from powerless to powerful. In what situations do you need to grow in confidence and courage? Which areas of your life will you lay down before God? How will you continue to press on to your reward?

Battle Cry for

Forgiveness

Days 12–14

My eyes are fixed on the cross. I overcome through Christ's forgiveness and resurrection!

Day 12

Embrace the Power

Battle Cry: *My eyes are fixed on the cross. I overcome through Christ's forgiveness and resurrection!*

> For if we have become united with Him in the likeness of His death, certainly we shall also be in the likeness of His resurrection.
> —Romans 6:5 (NASB)

Today we will focus our hearts and minds back on the basics. The scarlet blood of Christ cleanses us of unrighteousness, making us acceptable to God. We often hear the cliché "it's under the blood." This is absolutely true of our sins. They are washed away and we are given a clean slate. The Bible, in 1 John 1:9 (NASB), says, "If we confess our sins, He is faithful and righteous to forgive us our sins and to cleanse us from all unrighteousness." Keeping the communication lines open with God through confession and repentance is imperative to live an abundant life.

Yet let us not dismiss the gravity of Christ's sacrifice with deliberate, habitual sin. No, may it never be! In order to walk free and victorious in Christ, it is crucial that we understand how complete God's forgiveness is toward us. Scripture says that God's forgiveness extends for eternity, " ... as far as the east is from the west" (Psalm 103:12). Indeed, your "certificate of debt" has been canceled! (See Colossians 2:13–14.) It is because of forgiveness that we are qualified to stand in God's presence as His daughters! We are redeemed by Christ's blood, and grace is the gift lavished upon us (Ephesians 1:7). It is by this same grace that we walk in the power of the cross knowing that our trespasses are completely forgiven. We *must* realize His resurrection offers us the power to be victorious over sin.

Think of the term *resurrection power*. It's not found in Scripture, but it refers to the power of God that resurrected Jesus Christ from the tomb. Resurrect means to "raise from the dead." Jesus's body laid in the tomb, empty of life, yet on the third day the power of God brought Him back to life. Resurrection power. His resurrection was *for* you. Thus, His resurrection power is available *to* you! Jesus said to Martha, "I am the resurrection and the life; he who believes in Me will live even if he dies ..." (John 11:25a NASB). This is the promise for you and me: if we believe in Jesus, we

Day 12

will live even when we die! His death and resurrection provide us new life in Him. Although you are physically alive, perhaps you are spiritually or emotionally dead. Maybe your marriage or relationships seem lifeless. Maybe your unfulfilled dreams seem unreachable. Maybe your health is being challenged or threatened. His resurrection power gives you the authority to speak God's truth into your situations and see new life resurrect in them.

Jesus wants you to believe in resurrection power. It is your life source! Look at what He said in John 11:41–42 prior to calling Lazarus from his grave. " ... Then Jesus raised His eyes, and said, 'Father, I thank You that You have heard Me. I knew that You always hear Me; but because of the people standing around I said it, so that they may believe that You sent Me.'" Before raising Lazarus, Jesus acknowledged that *your* Father in heaven was the source of His resurrection power. In the same way, Jesus is ready to resurrect what is dead in your life. The same Father who called Jesus out of the grave is your Father.

Embrace the power of God that flows through your life to redeem your past and restore your future. Understand that forgiveness is available to you only through Christ's sacrifice of the cross. Victory is yours by Christ's sacrifice on the cross. Walk in that victory today!

Forgiveness

Intentional Thinking: You overcome by aligning yourself with the cross, walking in Christ's forgiveness and resurrection power. How would your life differ if you harnessed this resurrection power? Based on these truths, what are you going to tell yourself today?

Prayer: Thank You, Lord, for the cross. Thank You for forgiveness and resurrection. I am so grateful for the way You have made for me. I fix my eyes on You, Jesus. Today I embrace the resurrection power that is made available to me. I love You, Lord. In Jesus's name, amen.

For Further Study: John 3:16–18; Acts 4; Colossians 2:13–14; Psalm 145:17.

Day 13

Stay Fixed

Battle Cry: *My eyes are fixed on the cross. I overcome through Christ's forgiveness and resurrection!*

> … fixing our eyes on Jesus, the author and perfecter of faith, who for the joy set before Him endured the cross, despising the shame, and has sat down at the right hand of the throne of God.
> —Hebrews 12:2 (NASB)

Are your eyes fixed on Christ and His work on the cross? In order to overcome the obstacles in your life, you must stay fixed on the Lord and what His sacrifice means for you. The term "fixing our eyes" in this verse is translated from the Greek word *aphoraō*, which means to turn the eyes away from other things *and* fix them on something. It's a two-part action: *look away from* **and** *then look to Christ*. To fix your eyes on the author and perfecter of faith, you must remove your gaze from

Forgiveness

other things. What do you need to look away from to see Jesus?

This verse further speaks of the suffering Christ endured at the cross. What has the cross accomplished for you? This is where Christ laid down His rights and His life to bear the penalty of your sins. He endured the crucifixion for you and conquered sin and condemnation. Christ paid all penalties due for your past and future sins. Yesterday we reviewed Colossians 2:13–14, which tells us that Christ "nailed it [our debts] to the cross." Do you live in the reality of what Jesus endured for you on the cross? Oh, the joy of the cross!

Do you comprehend the magnitude of Christ's love for you that kept Him on the cross with nails in His hands? Fix your eyes and heart on the depths of His love and the power of grace in light of the cross. Christ's crucifixion fulfilled our debts. Do you know that if you align yourself with the cross you will be empowered to forgive others? You see, all of the forgiveness Jesus offers you is also available to others, even those who have wounded you. He is your source of power to live a life of forgiveness.

Jesus is the source of life in whatever you face. No matter who you need to extend forgiveness to today, He is the source of power to forgive. No matter where you need healing today, He is the source of that healing.

Stay fixed with your gaze on Him and the cross. Live in the power of Christ!

Intentional Thinking: The cross is your symbol of forgiveness, and you have access to the Lord's resurrection power to forgive others. What will you tell yourself today in light of God's forgiveness and His call for you to forgive?

Prayer: Lord, You are so kind and generous with Your grace. I am grateful for the unconditional love You freely give me. Give me Your heart, Lord. Empower me to release my offenders to You. Give me eyes to see them the way You do. I choose to forgive them. In Jesus's name, amen.

For Further Study: Luke 4:20; 1 Timothy 4:10; 5:5; 1 John 3:3.

Day 14

Overcomer

Battle Cry: *My eyes are fixed on the cross. I overcome through Christ's forgiveness and resurrection!*

> But in all these things we overwhelmingly conquer through Him who loved us.
> —Romans 8:37 (NASB)

God loves you! You were saved to overcome—both in your life and your calling! An overcomer is one who prevails in a struggle, one who conquers, one who defeats an opponent in a conflict. Here's some word trivia for you: both of the words *victorious* and *overcome* are the same Greek word *nikaō*, which means to conquer, to carry off the victory, to come out victorious. They are synonymous. You must get this truth in your mind and heart: you will not overcome if your heart is bound with resentment, anger and offense. You must live a lifestyle of forgiveness if you want to be an overcomer!

Day 14

What do you want to overcome in your life? Where do you need victory? Here are a few promises for you to stand on while you fight the good fight:

- **Victory is through Christ!** "The sting of death is sin, and the power of sin is the law; but thanks be to God, who gives us the victory through our Lord Jesus Christ." (1 Corinthians 15:56–57)
- **Christ proclaims He overcomes the world!** "These things I have spoken to you, so that in Me you may have peace. In the world you have tribulation, but take courage; I have overcome the world." (John 16:33)
- **Christ overcame death!** "But God raised Him up again, putting an end to the agony of death, since it was impossible for Him to be held in its power." (Acts 2:24)
- **Your faith in Christ is essential to your victory!** "For whatever is born of God overcomes the world; and this is the victory that has overcome the world—our faith." (1 John 5:4)

Just as your salvation comes by belief in your heart and confession with your mouth that "Christ is Lord" (Romans 10:9), your victory in this life comes by your belief and faith in Christ. Are you feeling victorious? Are you interceding for yourself? Do you live the lifestyle of forgiveness Christ mandates? Where trials and tribulation run rampant in your life, are you running to God for deliverance and strength to overcome?

If your answer is "No, I'm not feeling victorious," the solution is to become overwhelmed with the presence of God. The presence of God is first found through engaging with the Holy Spirit for the repentance of sin and commitment to holiness. Then, taking time for personal prayer and worship will open your eyes to His already existing presence. Jesus promises, "Lo, I am with you always, even to the end of the age" (Matthew 28:20 NASB). Sitting still, while waiting with an expectant heart, you will experience His presence resting upon you. Here you will be encouraged, healed, instructed, refreshed, and overwhelmed by His love and peace for you! The victory of an overcomer occurs in the heart—not in the circumstances. In His presence is where you'll find victory!

God never intended that you go through life alone. In fact, we have the Helper. The Holy Spirit dwells inside you to convince you of your identity and authority. Wrap your mind around this truth: one of the three persons of the triune God lives in you! Dwell on that! The Holy Spirit is the source of the resurrection power you need to overcome in your life. Walk in this knowledge daily in order to live the abundant life Jesus promises (John 10:10b). Align yourself with the cross; partner with the Holy Spirit in you; surrender to God's plan and will for your life. Remember that victory is the Lord's; thus, victory is yours. Live victoriously!

Intentional Thinking: You overcome by first fixing your eyes on the cross and then walking in your identity and authority. What will you do to experience God's presence today? Who do you need to forgive to embrace the lifestyle of forgiveness that Christ mandates? How can the Holy Spirit help you change your thinking about what you are facing? How will today's truths affect your mind-set?

Prayer: Lord, I am ready to overcome. Reveal where I need to surrender to Your power and Holy Spirit. I desire to align myself with the cross; show me how. I commit to seeking and finding Your presence. Today I line up with what You are doing in my heart. I agree with You, God, and submit to Your ways. I choose to forgive! In Jesus's name, amen.

For Further Study: Psalm 95; Matthew 5:23–24; Romans 8:37; Ephesians 5:1; 1 John 5:5; Revelation 2:7.

Your Turn

These last few days we've aimed to capture the power of the cross, the meaning of Christ's forgiveness and resurrection for the believer, and how it all makes way for you to overcome. Do you still struggle with accepting and receiving His forgiveness or extending forgiveness to others? Where do you need that resurrection power in your life? Are your eyes fixed on Jesus, or is something blocking your view? What can you do to live victoriously in Christ?

Battle Cry for

Forgiveness

Days 15–17

I walk in the confidence of Jesus Christ's love and mercy!

Day 15

No Condemnation

Battle Cry: *I walk in the confidence of Jesus Christ's love and mercy!*

> Therefore, there is now no condemnation for those who are in Christ Jesus.
> —Romans 8:1 (NASB)

Before you can really embrace the truth of God's constant love and unending mercy, you must disband the lies of the Enemy that keep you defeated. Satan, your enemy, is the accuser of the brethren (Revelation 12:10). *He comes to kill, steal and destroy* (John 10:10). If Satan can plague you by guilt, regret, and shame, he wins. Assaults on your character, accusations against you, and reminders of past mistakes are his weapons. His goal is to make you feel worthless. When you feel worthless, you lose your identity in Christ. (Remember: on Day 2 we learned we must not walk according to our

Forgiveness

feelings.) The Enemy uses condemnation to steal your power, weaken your faith, and extinguish your zeal for God's purpose for your life. Are you able to identify the condemnation from Satan? Can you discern his lies? Here's a clue: when guilt and shame are isolating you from the Lord, the Enemy is at work and lying to you!

Disowning lies from Satan is the best way to counterattack his condemnation. Victory comes by knowing the truth—knowing what God says about you and your future. This is at the heart of holding to a kingdom perspective. You must let the truth of Romans 8:1 sink deep into your heart and mind. Reread the verse above. Are you in Christ? If so, *there is no condemnation for you.* None!

Memorize 1 John 1:9: *If we confess our sins, He is faithful and righteous to forgive us our sins and to cleanse us from all unrighteousness.* Read the truth again: *He is faithful to forgive us*! So, then, with God's forgiveness and cleansing, there is no reason to believe you're condemned. When you are feeling condemned, take the opportunity to speak the truth into your heart and mind. Practice intentional thinking. Condemnation does not belong to you!

If reading and meditating on this truth doesn't convince you of your freedom in Christ, then is it possible your life includes some unconfessed sin, known or unknown? This verse in First John is your invitation to deal with it. Ask the Holy Spirit to reveal the sin to you;

Day 15

confess it and get it off your chest to the Lord. Once you do, it will no longer be a heavy burden. When we stay in a place of repentance and confessing our sins, we stay cleansed and free of condemnation.

Today is the day you embrace your freedom in Christ (Galatians 5:1). Take some time to search your heart before the Lord and ask Him to reveal anything that the Enemy has been lying to you about. It could be your identity, value, abilities, your past or future. Ask the Lord to tell you the truth about these things so you are armed to fight condemnation with the weapon you need—the truth. Walk in freedom today!

Intentional Thinking: Walk in the confidence in Christ's love and mercy. Can you identify any area that Satan tries to condemn you in? What does God have to say about that? How will you let these truths impact your thinking today?

Prayer: Thank You, Lord, for making a way for me to be free. I am grateful You cleanse me from unrighteousness when I confess my sin. Lord, show me the sin hiding in my heart. Empower me to repent and completely give up the sins that want to reign in my body and mind. I commit my heart and mind to You and claim freedom from guilt and shame. Condemnation does not belong to me! In Jesus's name, amen.

For Further Study: Romans 8.

Day 16

His Generous Love

Battle Cry: *I walk in the confidence of Jesus Christ's love and mercy!*

> For I am convinced that neither death, nor life, nor angels, nor principalities, nor things present, nor things to come, nor powers, nor height, nor depth, nor any other created thing, will be able to separate us from the love of God, which is in Christ Jesus our Lord.
> —Romans 8:38–39 (NASB)

Another truth necessary to know and believe as you walk confidently with the Lord is that *nothing can separate you from the love of God*. Nothing! It is imperative to have this truth of God's love bound to your mind and heart. Reflect on these truths about God's generous love:

- **God's love came first.** God is love. He initiates His love toward you. He loved you first. You

don't earn His love; it's His gift to you (1 John 4:7, 16, 19).
- **God's love is unchanging.** There is no wavering in God's heart for you. He loves unconditionally with full acceptance of who you are (Micah 7:18).
- **God's love is sacrificial.** Jesus's sacrifice on the cross was motivated by His love and desire for you to join Him in heaven (John 3:16; 15:13; Romans 5:8; Galatians 2:20).
- **God's love is everlasting.** There is no end to God's love for you. He never withdraws His love for you. It is boundless and eternal (Jeremiah 31:3).

Do you believe God loves you this much? In a world of conditional love, selfish motives, and rejection, you must not lose sight of how generous God's love is for you. God does not love us like humans do. People deny love to others for many reasons: failure, weakness, lack of talent or resources. The Lord does not love like men or women love. The Lord's eyes are on your heart ... *For God sees not as man sees, for man looks at the outward appearance, but the Lord looks at the heart* (1 Samuel 16:7).

Do you believe God will never stop loving you? Indeed, He *cannot* stop loving you. It is His nature to always and forever love you. This is truth. Understanding His complete and perfect love should further free you from fear, doubt, disbelief, and condemning thoughts. Our prayer is that God gives you a fresh revelation of God's love for you!

Consider how the Lord calls us to love one another. How can you do this if you have not embraced the depth of God's love for yourself? Reflecting on God's continuous love—regardless of your shortcomings—empowers you to love others beyond their shortcomings. His love motivates us to love Him as well as others in His name. Set a goal to fully comprehend God's love so that you can possess it enough to extend to others. God's love is an abundant resource for you. Daily keep your spiritual eyes and heart open for it!

Intentional Thinking: What will you tell yourself today about God's love for you? Will you live confidently in His love? How will these truths impact your relationships? Will you extend His love to others?

Prayer: Lord, thank You that Your love is unending, unfailing, and unlimited. Enable me to catch the vision of Your great love for me. Impress in my spirit how deep and wide is Your great love. I want to fully comprehend Your love, God, so that I can pour it out on others. May my words and deeds reflect Your love to those around me. In Jesus's name, amen.

For Further Study: Matthew 22:36–40; 1 Corinthians 13:4–7; Hebrews 6:10; 1 John 4:7.

Day 17

Mercy Every Day

Battle Cry: *I walk in the confidence of Jesus Christ's love and mercy!*

> He has shown you, O mortal, what is good. And what does the Lord require of you? To act justly and to love mercy and to walk humbly with your God.
> —Micah 6:8

Yesterday, did you keep your eyes open for signs of Christ's amazing love for you? We hope you saw it at every turn. Today we will talk more about that love and what can happen when you give it away! Mercy is goodness extended to another person when he or she doesn't deserve goodness; or mercy can involve extending goodness to someone in need of compassion or sympathy. Mercy is a trait of God that we don't talk about very much. As kingdom daughters, mercy should be an active part of how we approach our family, friends, and community. Indeed, nothing shows the heart of Jesus better than mercy.

Walking in God's forgiveness means you no longer walk in condemnation. As you align yourself with the cross, that same mercy for you is translated into mercy for others. We are never to condemn, but to show mercy. We see repeatedly in the gospels that Jesus healed those who came to Him. Just as Jesus lived a lifestyle of mercy, so are we to live a lifestyle of mercy. When you extend mercy with a kind gesture and genuine words, you will see another's countenance lifted and a light renewed in their eyes. Mercy is an extension of genuine concern for another. Stay alert for opportunities to extend mercy today!

But sometimes mercy is just harder than that. In times and situations of great pain, mercy is a challenge. Even in light of the cross and the undeserved mercy extended to you, it can be terribly difficult to even consider mercy in the face of your pain. But mercy isn't meant to come from feelings—it's a choice made in obedience. It's a choice to surrender *all* of yourself to Jesus. A choice to overcome your hurt through Christlike living. A choice to stand above your pain and act out of *who you are called to be* and *your* destiny. Do you remember what Jesus said of His accusers and tormenters? "Father, forgive them, for they do not know what they are doing" (Luke 23:34).

Day 17

Jesus was able to forgive His oppressors because He chose to view them through their weaknesses, not His broken heart and body. *He contended for them because of His identity.* If you must engage with someone you have forgiven, mercy allows you to respond to him or her from your identity in Christ, not from your wounds. Your offender may have damaged your heart, but such persons only damage your identity and affect your destiny if you allow them to. At these times, intentional thinking is crucial. Who will you choose to be, daughter of the Most High God?

Intentional Thinking: Life looks different when you walk with confidence in Christ's love and mercy. How will these truths affect your thinking? Can you think of opportunities you may have to be merciful today?

Prayer: Lord, my heart is amazed by Your generous love and mercy. I am so grateful that You continually extend Your merciful hand to me. I recognize that You desire me to be a vessel of Your mercy to those around me. Empower me today to do so. May my actions reflect my identity as Your daughter as I bear the fruit of mercy. I am merciful! In Jesus's name, amen.

For Further Study: Zechariah 7:9; Matthew 23:23; Luke 10:30–37; Hebrews 2:17; James 2:13.

Your Turn

Are you confident in God's love for you? Is condemnation blocking your view of God's generous love? How does His love for you help *you* show mercy to others? Are you living out of your identity in Christ, or are you stumbling through life, living out of your hurts? Write about these things and consider this statement: "I, like Jesus, choose a lifestyle of mercy."

Battle Cry for

Forgiveness

Days 18–20

**I forgive others and release them to Christ.
I receive His abundant healing!**

Day 18

I Forgive

Battle Cry: *I forgive others and release them to Christ. I receive His abundant healing!*

> Do not judge, and you will not be judged. Do not condemn, and you will not be condemned. Forgive, and you will be forgiven. Give, and it will be given to you. A good measure, pressed down, shaken together and running over, will be poured into your lap. For with the measure you use, it will be measured to you.
>
> —Luke 6:37–38

Over the next few days we are going to focus on this verse, for it has many depths to explore as we talk about forgiveness. With a simple read through today's Scriptures, we are reminded that people are, well, just people. Relationships are challenging for one reason—people! We are all born with the capacity to love and be loved. That same capacity gives us hope to risk engaging in relationships. However, when those same relationships struggle, we are quick to judge hearts and condemn behavior! Regardless of whether close relationships or just acquaintances are involved, opportunities to practice forgiveness arise on a regular basis.

Shouldn't it be easy for a Holy Spirit–filled Christian woman to extend forgiveness? After all, Christ forgives every day. The answer to that question is simple: No! It isn't always *easy* to forgive. Nowhere in Scripture does it say that forgiving is *easy*. Indeed, Jesus acknowledges the challenge of forgiveness when He says to forgive "seven times seventy" (Matthew 18:22). Why is Jesus so insistent? Because forgiveness of others is a kingdom principle! He knows that forgiveness is necessary for inner healing and intimate fellowship with Him. Laying down your wounded heart through forgiveness is the first step of healing. Remember this: while we live *on* this earth we are to live *by* the Holy Spirit and embrace the influences of the Lord's kingdom principles.

Look at it this way: forgiving is aligning with the cross. Our capacity to extend forgiveness is accessed by engaging with the power of the blood of Jesus, who forgives! Out of His great love and abandonment of His will, Jesus went to the cross for the sake of what? Forgiveness! His crimson blood overcame all sin, including the sin of the person who harmed you. His love that forgives is a most powerful force! That

Day 18

journey to the cross was difficult for Jesus, and your journey to forgive may be difficult as well. Will you do it anyway? If we are to be to this fallen world who Christ is to it, we must carry His heart to forgive others.

Aligning your life with the cross is a tall order! It means extending to others what God extended to you: forgiveness, grace, hope, and love. People hurt us, sometimes deeply! They don't typically set out to injure us, but they do. Each of us is called to choose a life of forgiveness—and it is a choice. Fortunately, a Christian doesn't live this life alone! The Holy Spirit is your Comforter, and He will hold you through the forgiveness process. He will speak the truth that overcomes the lies of your anger and pain, if you listen to Him. He will calm your fears, if you trust Him. He will show you how to embrace the perspective of heaven, if you lean on Him. Whatever you are receiving in your heart and soul by holding on to your hurts the Holy Spirit can heal.

If you are caught up in the sin of unforgiveness, choose to forgive, and set yourself free today. Engage the power of the blood of Christ in your life to forgive. He shed it to both forgive you and empower you to forgive others. If you can't forgive from your heart, forgive because of His heart. And tomorrow when that hurt resurfaces—do it again! Speak the truth to yourself and know that joy, peace, and abundance belong to you. Are you aligned with the cross? It's your choice.

Forgiveness

Intentional Thinking: Can you forgive and release your offenders to Christ in order to receive His healing? Aligning yourself with His work on the cross can revolutionize your attitude and thinking. How can these truths affect your mind-set and relationships?

Prayer: Thank You, Jesus, for the empowerment of the Holy Spirit to line up with what Scripture calls us to. Lord, give me the strength to let go of all my hurts to You. Thank you, Jesus, for the power of the Spirit to line up with God's call to forgive. Today, I choose to recognize You are the source of my ability to forgive. I choose forgiveness. In Jesus's name, amen.

For Further Study: Matthew 6:15; 18:35; Mark 4:12; Luke 11:4; 2 Corinthians 2:10; Colossians 3:13.

Day 19

I Release

Battle Cry: *I forgive others and release them to Christ. I receive His abundant healing!*

> Do not judge, and you will not be judged. Do not condemn, and you will not be condemned. Forgive, and you will be forgiven. Give, and it will be given to you. A good measure, pressed down, shaken together and running over, will be poured into your lap. For with the measure you use, it will be measured to you.
>
> —Luke 6:37–38

Forgiveness is the first step in healing from offenses and hurts, but it certainly isn't the last. The journey of healing requires releasing the person, the pain, and the consequences. The next step is the *decision* to release the judgment and condemnation held against your forgiven offender into God's capable hands. Yesterday, we mentioned aligning ourselves with the reality and power of the cross to forgive and taking up a kingdom perspective. Today we will look at the freedom that comes as we give up being judge and jury.

> Unforgiveness is like drinking poison and hoping the other person will die. (Debbie Ford)

Our verse in Luke points us to a very important spiritual law: we reap what we sow. Now, this isn't your typical use of the "reap what you sow" law, but it's very fitting when it comes to the subject of forgiveness. When we sow judgment and condemnation, we reap judgment and condemnation *upon ourselves*. Wouldn't it be much better to reap mercy? God's Word says that if we desire forgiveness, we must also forgive! (See Matthew 6:15.) And this is why forgiveness is for the *forgiver* not the *forgiven*! Extending mercy is the antidote for the poison of unforgiveness!

We know this already, don't we? So why do we have such a hard time putting this spiritual law into effect in our lives? Quick answer: emotions! Forgiveness is tricky business—it can feel empowering to hold something against someone, but indeed it is crippling. We tend to believe our emotions are truth. They are not truth! They are a response to our situation, but as we learned in Day 2, they are terrible assessors of truth. A struggle to forgive lies mostly with unsanctified anger. When we choose to partner with the anger (and the lies it tells us) instead of submitting it to the sanctification process, impurities and bitterness surface in our lives. We often mistake the feeling of anger for power. When angered, we feel righteous to judge and to determine the consequences of another's bad behavior. What we don't see is that this only piles upon us the responsibility to be the other's judge and jury—an even heavier weight. This is God's role—not ours!

You may be thinking, "If they only knew what I have suffered ..." God knows, and He loves you enough to hold you through your healing process. Release into God's very capable hands your offense, frustration, anger, fear, or whatever emotion is holding you back from forgiving. You can trust Him with your heart and with your offense. And you can also trust that He is patient and just (Psalm 145:8). He is waiting. Hold tight to the promise of His goodness as you release your offenders.

Intentional Thinking: Since God's healing comes when you forgive and release your offenders, will you begin the process of healing today? Will you trade the pain and anger in your heart for the loving touch of God and peace from the Holy Spirit? How will partnering with God change your life?

Prayer: Father, it isn't easy to forgive those who have deeply wounded me. However, I choose Your will to be free. By the power of the Holy Spirit, enable me to

Forgiveness

trust You, and empower my heart to forgive. Keep me steadfast in Your mercy and love today. I release to You those who have hurt me. In Jesus's name, amen.

For Further Study: Psalm 145.

Day 20

Free to Heal

Battle Cry: *I forgive others and release them to Christ. I receive His abundant healing!*

> Do not judge, and you will not be judged. Do not condemn, and you will not be condemned. Forgive, and you will be forgiven. Give, and it will be given to you. A good measure, pressed down, shaken together and running over, will be poured into your lap. For with the measure you use, it will be measured to you.
> —Luke 6:37–38

On this third day of proclaiming this battle cry, have an expectant heart! Do you desire the abundant life Jesus promises? From our verse in Luke, we find His abundance as the result of forgiving and releasing—extending the mercy that we too wish to have. God does not request us to forgive; God commands it! Once again, forgiveness is an act of obedience and trust in your Father! It brings about the redemption of our wounded hearts, which releases abundance. But what does it mean to have abundant healing?

Abundance of faith! You see, God knows the whole story. He knows what you do not, cannot! As the daughter of the King, you can partner with Him as He unfolds your story and "makes all things work for His glory" (Romans 8:28). Faith belongs to you! Allow the Holy Spirit to deposit truth into your heart! Truth that heals. Truth that frees. Truth that reveals God's goodness. Your forgiving heart opens the door for a deeper faith in Him. It's time to embrace this kingdom principle: trials lead to greater faith and endurance, which result in abundance (James 1:2–4). You will never be victorious if you don't fight a few battles! Everything you face in this life is an opportunity to see the miraculous healing grace of God. Abundant faith is an enviable gift!

Abundance of joy! Joy is that feeling of great happiness that comes with the best things in life! Perhaps you have heard people give their testimonies and you have seen them break into a huge smile when they get to the part that starts "And this is how God …" Joy is not just the result of your victory; it is also a crucial element that drives the healing process. Joy is not the absence of sadness; it is the presence of God's love, even in the midst of sadness. Your relationship with Him is the source for joy! Nehemiah 8:10 promises, "The joy of the Lord is our strength." Like the electricity you access when plugging a lamp into a socket, joy is an empowering resource that uplifts your heart. Joy is a fruit harvested from a mind set on Christ and things above. When you leave your burdens at the cross, you are open to receive fullness of joy! JOY: **J**esus **O**n **Y**ou!

Abundance of hope! There are few things that will extinguish hope quicker than the wounds of a broken heart. Failing hope brings on disappointment and discouragement. Hopelessness is a dark place, and Satan wants nothing more than to keep your "hoper" broken. It is crucial to understand that when you align yourself with the cross, disappointment and discouragement fade away. They are temporary and they *do not* belong to you. Hope is eternal and it *does* belong to you! Hope plays a powerful role in the healing you need! We exhort you to actively hope in Jesus and see how He brings restoration as you believe for a day that the hurt is no longer. As a Spirit-filled daughter of the Most High God, hope runs through your veins!

Which area of abundance do you desire to grasp today? Optimally, all of them! Faith, joy, and hope are at the very heart of God for you. He freely opens His heart and gives you an opportunity to be free! It's your choice though. If your heart is holding on to unforgiveness and all it comes with, you cannot grab ahold of God's blessings and abundance. If you try to hold on to resentment while reaching for His abundance, the best you will get is mediocrity. Jesus didn't die for you to have a mediocre life. He died to give you *abundance*. It's His gift to you!

Intentional Thinking: Do you desire the healing from Christ that comes from forgiving and releasing those who have hurt you? In light of the abundance of faith, joy, and hope available to you, how will you respond today? How will you allow these truths to change your thinking?

Prayer: Thank You, Father! I am deserving of nothing, yet in Your kindness, You offer me the abundance of everything I truly need. I surrender into Your hands those who have hurt me. And I surrender my hurts, for they are temporary. I will not allow what hurts me to rob me of Your abundance. Instead, I choose to walk in healing and freedom! Lord I receive faith, joy, and hope today! In Jesus's name, amen.

For Further Study: Matthew 11:28; Mark 11:25; Romans 8:28; Ephesians 3:20; Colossians 1:9–11.

Your Turn

Five years from now you will look back on this time of life and see how your response to it has affected you. What do you want to see? Who do you need to forgive? Would you like to exchange the weight of your wound for healing? Can you exchange the weight of being judge and jury for freedom, peace, and renewed hope? Will you align your heart with the cross and the power to forgive? How will abundance of faith, joy, and hope inspire healing for you?

Battle Cry for

Obedience

Days 21–23

Out of a grateful heart, I walk in obedience,
relying on God and the power of His love!

Day 21

An Obedient Life

Battle Cry: *Out of a grateful heart, I walk in obedience, relying on God and the power of His love!*

> But the Helper, the Holy Spirit, whom the Father will send in my name, he will teach you all things and bring to your remembrance all that I have said to you.
> —John 14:26

It is intriguing that Jesus says we will do greater works than even He did while on earth. How can we possibly do more than Him? When His three-year ministry came to its end, He commissioned us to carry His message to the world! He reached thousands; we are commissioned to reach millions! We are called to obedience, not for obedience's sake, but for the kingdom's sake. So, what does it take to live an obedient life?

We need power and clarity of mind to truly obey! Consider this: when Jesus was baptized and heaven opened, at which time the Spirit descended upon Him, it was then that He began a life of active ministry. He demonstrated the importance of partnering with the Holy Spirit, of having access to God in a great way. On the day of Pentecost, the Holy Spirit was ushered to earth in a new way and for a new purpose: to empower us to carry on where Jesus left off. The Holy Spirit made available a greater connection for God's children than ever before. The Holy Spirit plays several roles in our lives (counselor, comforter), but according to John 14:26 (ESV), He is also our helper. To help us do what? Obey!

Obedience trades the desires of your heart for the desire of God's heart. It can be inconvenient, uncomfortable, and even frightening! You may have a dozen questions. You might have run a certain scenario of obedience in your head a hundred times and found no possible good ending. This is when you remember one crucial fact about your life: *it doesn't belong to you any longer!* When you said "Jesus is Lord" at the cross, you traded your life for His life in you! He is now your Master and Owner! (See Colossians 2:13.) If you remember that God is good and that His love overcomes, then obeying Him is really the only choice!

God is the most dependable entity in your life! You really can rely on Jesus and His love, power, and grace to guide you as you walk in obedience. Scripture promises that *you will receive power when the Holy Spirit has come upon*

Day 21

you (Acts 1:8). Dependence on the Holy Spirit is your source of strength and your safety net as you proceed! Failure comes with inaction—not inaccurate action! As you pray and seek guidance, know that He has a plan to prosper and mature you. What we accomplish through our obedience is less important than obedience itself. And obedience is its own reward because it matures you and glorifies God!

> ... so that the tested genuineness of your faith—more precious than gold that perishes though it is tested by fire—may be found to result in praise and glory and honor at the revelation of Jesus Christ. (1 Peter 1:7)

God has a lot to accomplish in His kingdom, and He desires to use your life to impact it! You can trust Him! You can trust the Holy Spirit to empower you to do all that God calls you to do. It will be an adventure. Are you ready for it?

Intentional Thinking: Is it a new concept for you that God's power and love enable you to obey Him? What will you tell yourself that will foster your obedience? How will the truths presented today change the way you view obedience?

Prayer: Lord, I truly choose You. I choose You to be my Savior and Lord. Remove any misunderstandings about why obedience is necessary. Please stop the lies of the Enemy that discourage obedience to Your Word and Spirit. I commit to obedience because I understand that it partners with Your will, protection, and love. Today, Lord, I partner with the Holy Spirit. In Jesus's name, amen.

For Further Study: 1 Samuel 15:22; 1 Thessalonians 1:4–7; Romans 6:11; 15:13; Colossians 3:1.

Day 22

A Grateful Heart

Battle Cry: *Out of a grateful heart, I walk in obedience, relying on God and the power of His love!*

> If you love me, you will keep my commandments.
> —John 14:15

Gratitude is powerful. We think of gratitude as a place where our heart is bowed to the mercy, generosity, or kindness shown to us, a place of appreciation of the love we desire and values we hold dear. God has rescued, redeemed, and restored us time and time again as we stroll through life! His mercy and compassion are overwhelmingly good to us! King David understood the power of both recognizing and acknowledging God's gracious ways.

> Then King David went in and sat before the Lord and said, "Who am I, O Lord God, and what is my house, that you have brought me thus far?" (2 Samuel 7:18)

Obedience

From our Scripture in John today, we see obedience as loving Jesus back. We sing songs of thankfulness and acknowledge how great God is. We utter "Praise the Lord" for everything from finding twenty dollars on the ground to a physical healing. But the true test of gratitude is not in speaking of it, but responding to it. Gratitude is so much more than lip service. It is a state of your heart that leads to obedience. Obedience is your gratitude in action!

What motivates you to obey? Is it to receive from Him? You may never see the fruit of your obedience, but know that your treasures and rewards are locked up in heaven, awaiting your arrival. "But store up for yourselves treasures in heaven, where moths and vermin do not destroy, and where thieves do not break in and steal" (Matthew 6:20). This is not to say that God doesn't reward obedience. He does and in enormous fashion! Indeed, the reward of obedience to the commandment to love and serve God is abundance! (See Deuteronomy 11:13.)

Or does your obedience come from a place of gratitude and a choice to live a life reflective of your identity in Christ? Do you obey to stay in line with your calling and in the authority of your position in the kingdom? Obedience tells God and the world where your allegiance is. You have been empowered through knowledge from the Word and Holy Spirit to know and walk in your calling. In Scripture, 2 Peter 1:3–11 speaks of this. In short, the following qualities result

Day 22

in an obedient life: virtue, knowledge, steadfastness, godliness, self-control, brotherly affection, and love.

If you desire to live a life that embraces all that God has for you, if you desire to hear those most coveted words, "Well done, my good and faithful *daughter*," then take a position of gratitude by making obedience your priority. Trust your Father to lead you in His ways; lean on the understanding that comes by communing with the Holy Spirit. Love Jesus and keep His commands.

Intentional Thinking: Relying on God's power and love in order to respond to commands with obedience is our goal. Is this easier when you connect obedience to having a grateful heart for His work on the cross for you? How will you keep your mind-set focused on gratitude and obedience today?

Prayer: Thank You, Lord, for all the abundance available to me. Change my heart, thoughts, and attitude today. Enable me to line up with Your commands with gratitude and praise from the heart. Lord, my heart cries out for more of You. Stay near to me, be patient with me, and please energize my obedience with the power of the Holy Spirit. I love You, Lord, and will obey You. In Jesus's name, amen.

For Further Study: John 10:10; 2 Peter 1:3–11; Colossians 1:5; Deuteronomy 28:1.

Day 23

Propelled by Love

Battle Cry: *Out of a grateful heart, I walk in obedience, relying on God and the power of His love!*

> Let your eyes look directly forward, and your gaze be straight before you.
> —Proverbs 4:25

On Day 21 we looked at the idea of reliance on the Holy Spirit to exchange your desires for His desires for the sake of the kingdom. Yesterday, we studied gratitude's power to inspire you to obey. The last step in embracing this battle cry is to understand that you are created to serve God. The power of His love for you can fuel your decision to obey.

Life is perpetually in forward motion: you can't stop it! However, your growth in Christ will cease with disobedience. Life is short. Today you can decide to remain in—or return to—a forward momentum in

Day 23

your journey with God. Consider this consequence to disobedience found in Jeremiah 7:24: "But they did not obey or incline their ear, but walked in their own counsels and the stubbornness of their evil hearts, and went backward and not *forward*" (emphasis added). May it never be said of us that we have a stubborn, evil heart. Instead, may we incline our ears to the voice of God and move forward in obedience.

God's love has the power to propel you into your destiny. Obedience is the pathway to the abundant life! Keeping your heart open and your thoughts submitted are vital to discovering all that God has for your life. Frankly, you have two choices. You can choose God's way, which is to *trust His love*, depend on the Holy Spirit through your sanctification process, align yourself with the cross, and regard the perspective of heaven over yours. Or you can choose the circular path of disobedience, which will undoubtedly hold you back from the promise of abundance Christ offers. The path of disobedience will become a rut that consumes you. Decide today that your life will be propelled forward by God's amazing love for you.

> Keep your heart with all vigilance, for from it flow the springs of life. Let your eyes look directly forward, and your gaze be straight before you. Ponder the path of your feet; then all your ways will be sure. (Proverbs 4:23, 25–26)

We pray that you do not allow Satan—continually accusing—to steal this moment from you with guilt or condemnation. Remember: condemnation does not belong to you! (See Day 15.) Instead, we hope your heart is rallied to enter into a deeper, richer relationship with God. If you want all He has for you, then you must follow Him! The apostle Paul had a keen understanding of the power of forward momentum. He said, in Philippians 3:12–14 (ESV), " ... but I press on to make it my own, because Christ Jesus has made me his own. ... forgetting what lies behind and straining forward to what lies ahead, I press on toward the goal for the prize of the upward call of God in Christ Jesus."

If Paul were here in person, likely he would inspire you to think with intention. He would exhort you to have a determined spirit and choose obedience! He goes on in verse 15 to say, "Let those of us who are mature think this way, and if in anything you think otherwise, God will reveal that also to you." Remember our primary example, Jesus: everything He did on this earth was in response to the Father He loved. John 5:19 says, *Jesus gave them this answer: "Very truly I tell you, the Son can do nothing by himself; he can do only what he sees his Father doing, because whatever the Father does the Son also does."*

There is no power on earth worthy of your complete abandon outside of the amazing, consuming love of God. May you be inspired to be healed and made whole, encouraged to walk in bold obedience, and propelled by love into your place in the kingdom. May God's love propel you with forward momentum every day!

Intentional Thinking: Are you convinced that you have the power to obey the Lord through His power and love? Has your heart become filled with gratitude for His love and the work on the cross even more so? How will your thinking line up with the truths shared today?

Prayer: Thank You, Lord, that You are willing and able to empower me to obey and serve You. I understand that obedience opens my life to the abundance of all You have waiting for me, here on earth and in heaven. I take authority over my thinking. Lord, quicken my spirit to obey and trust You even more than I've ever experienced. I will be obedient! In Jesus's name, amen.

For Further Study: Deuteronomy 30:1–5; Romans 6:17; 1 Peter 1:2; 1 John 2:5–6.

Your Turn

As you reflect back on the last three days, what do you notice that the Lord revealed to you about your life of obedience? What mind-sets keep you from living a surrendered life? Are you ready to challenge them by the power of the Spirit, overflowing gratitude, and intentional thinking? In what way will you choose a life of obedience today?

Battle Cry for

Obedience

Days 24–26

I submit to the sanctification process of the Holy Spirit!

Day 24

Sanctification

Battle Cry: *I submit to the sanctification process of the Holy Spirit!*

For this is the will of God, your sanctification …
—1 Thessalonians 4:3a (NASB)

Salvation is by your faith in Jesus Christ (Ephesians 2:8). Sanctification comes by your cooperation with the Holy Spirit, as He convicts and guides you toward freedom and transformation. Because of the cross your sins are removed, yet your attitudes, behaviors, habits, and thinking need to be eternally changed (see Day 12). Our mind-sets are changed when we release our opinions and thoughts to the Lord and embrace Him as the Truth (as the Word of God) and embrace His ways.

Why is this important? Why should you endure this process? Because you are destined *to become conformed to the image of His Son* (Romans 8:29). It is God's will that your flesh cease to control your actions and that His Spirit take over. The Holy Spirit will drive and purify your intentional thinking as you submit to this process.

The sanctification journey is similar to the process of purifying gold. In order for 10 karat gold to become 24 karat gold, it must be heated up over and over again. Each time the fire is turned up, the gold is melted to liquid, and the impurities come to the surface to be removed. To become finer, higher quality gold, the gold must submit to the fire and let the impurities be burned away. Liquid gold can be poured into any mold, being made into anything the goldsmith desires. God is your Goldsmith. He wants to form you into the image of His Son. But only by your submission to circumstances that heat you up—and bring your impurities to the surface—can you be purified and sanctified.

When situations occur in your life, do you respond lovingly, patiently, and graciously? Or do you respond out of offense, anger, fear, or depression? Situations that bring the impurities to the surface are "the Refiner's fire" (Malachi 3:2–3). When you feel the refining heat, realize this is the sanctification process in action. The humble response is to repent of sinful attitudes and reactions, seek the Holy Spirit's guidance, and depend on God's help to change.

The sanctification process takes us from living in the flesh to living by the Spirit. Galatians 5:25 calls us *to keep in step with the Spirit.* The more you submit, the clearer your discernment for decisions, situations, and relationships. It is a day by day process, all intended to transform you from glory to glory (2 Corinthians 3:16–18).

Every day we have opportunities to realize our impurities that need to be removed. Over the next couple of days, we're going to see how the Holy Spirit helps us through this process. Also, we'll look at our role of submission and obedience to that process. Your transformation comes with agreeing in the Spirit with the Word of God. Embrace the sanctification process!

Intentional Thinking: Today reflect on any attitudes, habits, or behaviors you believe God would like to refine and sanctify. After reading today's truths, do you find yourself submissive to the sanctification process? How will you line your life up with the Scriptures shared?

Prayer: Thank You, Lord, that I am not in this alone. I have You to guide and strengthen me through this process of sanctification. Empower me today to submit when the Holy Spirit is directing my thoughts, words, and actions. I invite You into my heart to continue the refining process. In Jesus's name, amen.

For Further Study: Job 22:21; Proverbs 3:6; James 4:7; 1 Thessalonians 4:3.

Day 25

Holy Spirit's Role

Battle Cry: *I submit to the sanctification process of the Holy Spirit!*

> But the Helper, the Holy Spirit, whom the Father will send in My name, He will teach you all things ...
> —John 14:26 (NASB)

The Holy Spirit, the third person of our triune God, is our guide through the sanctification process. And of course this is so—He is the Spirit that is *holy*! His goal to mature us from the "old man" toward holiness, which is what God calls us to (1 Peter 1:15–16). Does this standard of holiness overwhelm you?

How does the Holy Spirit help us in the process of sanctification? John 16:13 (NASB) says, *Jesus told His disciples, "But when He, the Spirit of truth, comes, He will guide you into all the truth; for He will not speak on His own initiative, but whatever He hears, He will speak; and He will disclose to you what is to come."* Let's consider this verse's implications.

1. **The Holy Spirit guides you into all truth.** Knowing the truth is key to Christian living. The truth is what sets you free from sin, entanglements with this world, and strongholds from your past (John 8:32).
2. **The Holy Spirit speaks what He hears from the Father.** When we dwell on the truth, we hear from the Holy Spirit and we are fixing our minds on the Father's heart toward us. This enables us to make choices that line up with His will for our lives. The Holy Spirit is our lifeline to the Father in heaven.
3. **The Holy Spirit discloses to you what is to come.** We must be in prayer and available to the Holy Spirit's downloads of information to us. God knows what is around the corner in our lives. If you will be still, He will prepare your heart. The Holy Spirit will disclose to you what to do next. Prayer is our opportunity to hear from the Holy Spirit to make decisions that are in alignment with God's perfect will for our lives.

The Holy Spirit also convicts us of sin (John 16:13). The Holy Spirit gives you that gut check when you're doing something you shouldn't. You know that feeling.

In certain conversations, the Holy Spirit says, "Share this," or "Don't say that—not good." On Friday nights, when your friends invite you to accompany them to a party or the movies, the Holy Spirit may say, "Don't go there—not good." You move toward the temptation of old sin, and the Holy Spirit says, "Don't pick up that sin again—not good." He convicts us. We feel that gut check. We need to listen to it. Scripture exhorts us to love God's discipline (Proverbs 12:1). Blessed are you if you receive correction (Job 5:17). If you love knowledge, you are wise (Proverbs 19:20).

Conviction is like the bumps on the highway when you begin to steer off course. The Holy Spirit is constantly at work to keep us on the road that leads to our holy calling in the Lord. The Holy Spirit's goal in all this speaking to us, convicting us, guiding us is *sanctification*. It is up to you to partner with Him, obey His instruction, and become all that God created you to be! Remember our verse John 14:26? We pray you will accept the Helper's guidance today.

Intentional Thinking: The goal is to submit to the sanctification process. You do this by consulting with and submitting to the Holy Spirit regarding your life, decisions, and relationships. What will you do with the valuable resource you have in the Holy Spirit, your loving Helper? How will this reality affect your thoughts today?

Prayer: Thank You, Holy Spirit, that You are available at all times. I desire the abundant life that You have for me. Keep my footing steady on the path of overcoming. I yield my spirit to Your sanctification process. Give me ears to hear You speak, convict, and guide. Increase my fruit of self-control so I freely submit. In Jesus's name, amen.

For Further Study: Isaiah 57:15; Matthew 3:11; Luke 12:12; Acts 1:8.

Day 26

Your Role

Battle Cry: *I submit to the sanctification process of the Holy Spirit!*

> ... but like the Holy One who called you, be holy yourselves also in all your behavior; because it is written, "You shall be holy, for I am holy."
> —1 Peter 1:16 (NASB)

Essential to the sanctification process is your pursuit of the Lord in prayer, the Word, and the Holy Spirit. The Lord desires you to separate yourself from your sin nature to abide in His holy nature. This requires action on your part. We are called to be doers of the Word (James 1:22). Will you embrace a life that is Spirit led in your decisions and behaviors?

Holiness is possible! Self-control is fruit of the Spirit (Galatians 5:22–23). It is key to holiness. In Scripture, 2 Timothy 1:7 (NASB) says, *For God has not given us a spirit*

Day 26

of timidity, but of power and love and discipline. Yesterday, we discussed the Holy Spirit's role in our sanctification. Yet we must also cooperate with and submit to Him. Daily, we must deny ourselves, pick up our cross, and follow Jesus (Luke 9:23). Yes! Deny yourself the things that feed your flesh. What weaknesses lead to sin in your life? What can you do to stop falling into the trap? The answer: *Submit therefore to God. Resist the devil and he will flee from you* (James 4:7 NASB).

What does this look like? When temptation knocks on the door, don't open it! Don't even go near it. Do everything by the power of the Holy Spirit and through prayer to *not give in*. If you endure the temptation, refuse to sin, and submit to God instead, that temptation will soon leave and you will be free. You may have to fight that battle a few times before you find yourself unmoved by what formerly enticed you. Putting James 4:7 into practice communicates to the Enemy that you are submitted to God, no longer in bondage to that sin because Jesus has empowered you to overcome, and you choose holiness instead. Know that freedom belongs to you!

You must partner with the Holy Spirit and comply with what He is doing in you to reach your abundant destiny. Strengthen those obedience muscles to be strong. Refuse to surrender to the sin. Don't pick up old sins; pick up your Bible. Don't continue with the former sinful habits of your "old man," but create for yourself a new spiritually energizing lifestyle. God's grace and love give you an escape from sin (1 Corinthians 10:13). You *must* take the escape route He offers and press on through the sanctification process. Shout your battle cry and stand your ground for holiness!

Intentional Thinking: Submitting to the sanctification process is for our own good. It releases the abundant goodness of God in your life. Are you catching the vision of the power of holiness? How will you align yourself with the sanctification process today?

Prayer: Lord, I submit to Your authority. Spring forth Your power in my life today as I deny myself, pick up my cross, and follow You. You are Lord over my choices, thoughts, emotions, and actions. I declare You as King above all. I will live in You and through Your power. In Jesus's name, amen.

For Further Study: 1 Samuel 15:22; Psalm 19:13; 37:37; 84:11; Philippians 2:15; 1 Thessalonians 3:13.

Your Turn

What behaviors or habits in your life are stifling your spiritual growth, your sanctification? What has the Holy Spirit convicted your heart to change? Do you trust Him to pour His goodness into your life? How will you submit to the process of sanctification? What temptations will you refuse? What behaviors will you choose to stop? What truths do you need to embrace to fulfill God's desire for holiness in your life?

Battle Cry for

Obedience

Days 27–29

**I surrender to God's Word and Spirit.
Holiness and humility are my standard!**

Day 27

The Choice to Surrender

Battle Cry: *I surrender to God's Word and Spirit. Holiness and humility are my standard!*

> Jesus answered, " ... and you shall love the Lord your God with all your heart, and with all your soul, and with all your mind, and with all your strength."
>
> —Mark 12:30 (NASB)

If you recall, on Day 22 we talked about obedience through gratitude and John 14:15, where Jesus says, "If you love me, you will keep my commandments." Obedience is also the result of surrendering and abandoning yourself to His plans. If you don't surrender, you simply will not be obedient. In this sense surrender means to yield to the possession and power of another. Surrender is the basis for all life and freedom in Christ. Let's start today by looking at God's promise for a surrendered mind.

> The mind governed by the flesh is death, but the mind governed by the Spirit is life and peace. (Romans 8:6)

Oh, to have a mind governed by life and peace! Learning to have a surrendered mind is a journey, or more accurately, a process. Sanctification involves surrendering your old thoughts and embracing God's thoughts. This is what it means to have a kingdom perspective. But there are more factors involved here than just the mind. Contending with one's willpower and heart are also important.

Ever had an experience like the following? You make a decision: "From this day on, I will/will not (fill in the blank)." But you turn right around to do the exact opposite. Well, you are in good company, as the apostle Paul had the same problem! In writing about overcoming sin, he said, "I do not understand what I do. For what I want to do I do not do, but what I hate I do" (Romans 7:15). This is where the battle of the wills comes in: your will versus God's will, the flesh versus the Spirit. Paul goes on to say, in verse 25, that only by God's law does he find what he needs to begin transforming his mind. It is crucial that you don't just read the Word, but surrender to the Word. Pray about it. Ponder it. Pray about it some more. Seek to *understand* God's Word, not just *know* His Word. A surrendered mind comes from

Day 27

- constantly submitting to the influence of the truth through reading the Word;
- recognizing that only Jesus overcomes our flesh;
- responding to the promptings of the Holy Spirit; and
- *actively* choosing to follow Him!

As your relationship with Jesus develops, your mind will further surrender to His will. We have struggles every single day! Hold tight to this concept: your enemy can convince you with his lies *only* when you don't know the truth! Thus, know the truth and embrace God's thinking.

As to the issue of the heart: Your emotions play a powerful role in your life. Emotions are never to be ignored, but always to be considered as unreliable revealers of the truth. Jesus wants to heal your emotions, but this takes submitting them to the tender care of the Holy Spirit. If you want a healthy heart, submit your emotions to the influence of the truth and not to the world or your circumstances. Submit emotions to the influence of your identity and calling in Christ, not to your desires and dreams, lest disappointment steal your joy and contentment. Submit emotions not to what you or anyone else deems your value and worth, but to God's opinion! If you question your value to Jesus, read Romans 8:38–39. You will discover that there is *nothing* that can separate you from God's love for you. It is this love that makes you valuable!

Choosing to surrender your mind will position you to walk in peace and authority. If you want to stand tall in the kingdom—bend your knee! Job 22:12 says, "Submit to God and be at peace with Him; in this way prosperity will come to you." Surrender your mind, your will, and your heart to His lovingkindness, and you will find obedience a natural response to your Father.

Intentional Thinking: Holiness and humility are the by-products of a heart surrendered to God's Word and Spirit. What behaviors will change as you let these truths influence you? How will living with a surrendered mind impact your life?

Prayer: Lord, continue with me on this journey of sanctification and surrender. I am grateful You are always at work in my heart and mind. Today I surrender myself to Your Word and Spirit. I declare a deeper commitment to You as I partner with the Holy Spirit to abide in Your presence and will. Keep me in step with You, Lord. In Jesus's name, amen.

For Further Study: Romans 8:5–11; 8:38–39; John 1:1; Hebrews 4:12; 1 Corinthians 15:2.

Day 28

A Holy Pursuit

Battle Cry: *I surrender to God's Word and Spirit. Holiness and humility are my standard!*

> Blessed be the God and Father of our Lord Jesus Christ, who has blessed us with every spiritual blessing in the heavenly places in Christ, just as He chose us in Him before the foundation of the world, that we would be holy and blameless before Him.
> —Ephesians 1:3–4 (NASB)

Did you catch the message in today's Scripture? Read the verses from Ephesians again, out loud. Let these words settle in your spirit, mind, and heart. The passage says, "just as He chose us ... that we would be holy." God chose us—imperfect, evil hearted, prideful, willful, and idolatrous people—to be His holy people. It was His design from the beginning that His children would echo His holiness. You were chosen to worship Him through holiness in spite of your humanity—which, by the way, doesn't deter or surprise Him! He sets the impossible standard that only in holiness can we stand before Him. Thank you, Father, for providing the way of holiness!

It is only through Jesus that holiness is even conceivable. Let's go back to our Scripture: "who has blessed us with *every* spiritual blessing in the heavenly places in Christ" (emphasis added). It is because of the covenant relationship with Jesus that access to the blessings of heaven, the resources of heaven, are possible for our lives today! Out of His kindness and great love for you, God makes the impossible standard of holiness possible through faith in Jesus Christ (Romans 10:10). Jesus took your sins upon Himself. At the cross, He also overcame your sin nature to present you as righteous and blameless. He has qualified you to stand before the throne of God! Praised be the name of Jesus and the power of His blood, without which holiness is an unimaginable goal.

> I have been crucified with Christ; and it is no longer I who live, but Christ lives in me; and the life which I now live in the flesh I live by faith in the Son of God, who loved me and gave Himself up for me. (Galatians 2:20 NASB)

Christ lives in you; everything you need for a life of holiness resides in you. This is why a relationship with the Holy Spirit is a crucial part of life (John 14:26). Without Him, you are limited; with Him, you have access

Day 28

to the power of heaven and the authority to live a holy life. It begins with recognition and acknowledgment of Christ's sacrifice and His overcoming of the world (John 16:33).

Yesterday, we discussed having a surrendered mind. This is a foundational principle of holiness that bears repeating. A surrendered mind comes from constant submission to the influence of the truth through reading the Word. We must recognize that only Jesus overcomes our flesh. To stay surrendered, we must respond to the promptings of the Holy Spirit and *actively* choose to follow Him!

Stop and think: Is holiness in the forefront of your mind? Or are you focusing on your worries and grumbling about the unfairness of life? Are you entertaining ungodliness or dwelling on what tempts you? Do your emotions sidetrack your pursuit of holiness? This kind of thought life will result in unhealthy thinking patterns. You will certainly be distracted away from the kingdom perspective you need in order to overcome. Do you spend more time confessing your sins than you do rejoicing in having overcome them? You should be aligning your heart with the cross by meditating on the goodness of God, the promises of His Word, and the potential for a life fulfilled through communion with the Holy Spirit. Holiness is a state of being, a condition of your current standing with Jesus. Holiness is such a huge part of living the abundant life Jesus came to give you; fight for it! May the pursuit of holiness be your standard!

Intentional Thinking: As you surrender in holiness and humility, are you prayerfully surrendering your distractions and temptations into Jesus's capable hands? How will these truths today affect your response to what life brings you?

Prayer: Thank You, Lord, that You reign over all. I surrender myself to You today. I give You my distractions because You guide me. I acknowledge what tempts me; show me the escape You have provided. I commit to obey and surrender to Your Word and Spirit. I pursue holiness. In Jesus's name, amen.

For Further Study: Psalm 19:14; 119:97; Romans 8:5–11; John 14:15–26.

Day 29

The Garment of Humility

Battle Cry: *I surrender to God's Word and Spirit. Holiness and humility are my standard!*

> For the Lord takes delight in his people; he crowns the humble with victory.
> —Psalm 149:4

There are so many things to be said about humility. Have you ever had one of those moments when the frailty of your best thinking and the immaturity of your heart become so, so evident? That moment you respond so poorly to something that your only prayer is "Please, God, I hope nobody saw this 'Jesus Loves You' T-shirt I'm wearing!" At these times your humanity smacks you in the face and the necessity for God's redeeming and restoring power becomes so obvious. Humility is a foundational part of living in God's grace, favor, and power so as to overcome and to serve. Let's look at two topics associated with humility: pride and servanthood.

God desires to bless you with victory that comes from humility. There are few things that dam up the streams of blessing and victory in life like pride! Our Scripture tells us that the Lord delights in humility. Bending your knee to His ways (submitting your mind, your heart, and your will) reaps a spiritual abundance in your life. The Word says that God longs for the spirit He placed in you; this is why He extends much grace to us. He knows how difficult humility can be. Scripture encourages humility by saying, "God opposes the proud but shows favor to the humble" (James 4:5–6). If we allow our own ideas, even our noble and good intentions, to trump God's ideas, then we have exalted ourselves above Him. We all know the old adage "Pride goes before the fall." It is true! Exalting yourself will lead to humiliation (Matthew 23:12). God longs to be the source of victory in your life. The glory belongs to Him! He can only have it if you allow Him to teach you and love you into His ways. Indeed, humility itself is evidence of His victory in your life.

We are all called to servanthood. Jesus came to serve; we are here to serve (Mark 10:45). At the risk of sounding harsh: it is only in humility that you can be fully useful to Him and serve others. God had a brilliant idea when He created you! He adorned you with your personality, strengths, talents, and capacities.

Day 29

God even has purposes for the weaknesses He's allowed in your nature. He did this not only for your life but also for your potential impact in His kingdom. You were created to love God and make a difference in this world by serving others. Humility both fuels and elevates your ability to serve.

> Therefore, as God's chosen people, holy and dearly loved, clothe yourselves with compassion, kindness, humility, gentleness and patience. (Colossians 3:12)

These are the necessary garments of all relationships: *compassion, kindness, humility, gentleness, and patience.* Who do these words describe? Yes, Jesus! If you are wearing these garments, you will reflect the love of Jesus to those around you. It is with these garments that you can be truly useful to Him. This is the heart of God: "Be completely humble and gentle; be patient, bearing with one another in love" (Ephesians 4:2). Partnering a rich understanding of the Word with the Holy Spirit, you are able to serve others with love and grace that comes from the Father. Consider yourself "on assignment" in the kingdom. These garments are the uniform by which the world will recognize you! Like holiness, is humility your standard?

Intentional Thinking: Are you ready to glorify God by surrendering in holiness and humility? Is pride speaking loudly in your life? Does the world see God's glory in your humility as you serve Him? How will you align your thinking with His Word and Spirit today?

Prayer: Lord, thank You again and again for the power of the Holy Spirit who enables me to do all that You are calling me to do. I agree with Your plans for my life. I agree with Your Word and Spirit. I commit to becoming more humble in my relationships and accomplishments. I commit to You as Lord of my life. Humility is my standard. In Jesus's name, amen.

For Further Study: Proverbs 15:33; John 14:15–26; Romans 7:6; 8:5–11; James 3:13.

Your Turn

How might life change if your mind was governed by the mind of Christ? How might your behaviors change when your heart is surrendered and holiness is your goal? Are you willing and ready to surrender your emotions, distractions, and temptations into Jesus's capable hands? What will you do differently today in response to Jesus's call to humility?

Day 30

The Final Day: Warrior On!

> Fight the good fight of the faith. Take hold of the eternal life to which you were called when you made your good confession in the presence of many witnesses.
> —1 Timothy 6:12

You made it! It is Day 30! Thank you for spending this last month with us. We hope you are enjoying the rewards that come when you choose to live your life powerfully surrendered to the Holy Spirit and when you choose to think with intention based on truth. The shout of a true warrior comes from a deep place of conviction and determination to overcome any and all challenges. She runs into her battles armed with faith and convinced of God's victory!

On Day 1, we began this journey by looking at Isaiah 42:13, where we see the Lord shouting His battle cry and triumphing over His enemies. The Lord stirs Himself up. In other words, He prepares and engages

Day 30

His heart into action. Then He raises the battle cry with a shout!

Together, we have journeyed through the Word to discuss many topics and explore many truths. Some of the topics have been chosen to remind you of the foundational truths we embrace and engage in as Christians; others were chosen to deepen your understanding and challenge you to embrace a kingdom perspective in a fresh way. It is in knowing and believing God's Word that you have the authority to speak and respond out of truth, not circumstances or emotions!

Do you recall the advice from Day 2? "Be very careful what you tell yourself about how you feel." This is the basis of intentional thinking! Here, again, are the three keys to positioning yourself to respond to and overcome your emotions:

1. Understand that emotions aren't necessarily right or wrong and that they are terrible assessors of the situation at hand.
2. Speak the truth, which comes from knowing Jesus, the Truth, the Word of God.
3. Put on the "new self" and decide to think differently.

We are called to triumph by following God's lead! This will require you to embrace the truth, decide what you will tell yourself, and take action based on that

Obedience

truth. You have been presented with nine battle cries, all designed to give you opportunities to engage in the power of intentional thinking and align yourself with the cross. Let's read, once more, the verses that inspire us into action and show the promise of Jesus, the ultimate overcomer. We pray you embrace them with your mind and write them on your heart!

> The Lord will march out like a champion, like a warrior he will stir up his zeal; with a shout he will raise the battle cry and will triumph over his enemies. (Isaiah 42:13)

> I have told you these things, so that in me you may have peace. In this world you will have trouble. But take heart! I have overcome the world. (John 16:33)

Has there been a transformation in your thinking since Day 1? Have you taken up the opportunity to speak truth into your life? We hope each day has built up your faith, encouraged your heart, sharpened your thinking, inspired a deeper connection with the Holy Spirit, and equipped you to be the overcomer that you are. If you have embraced your identity and the intention of the nine battle cries, you are surely stronger and more fortified! We pray that you have put the truths to work in your life, your mind is clearer, and your warrior heart has been ignited.

Before we close and turn this over to you and God, here is one more verse for you to meditate on. What areas of your life would radically change if this was a truth on which you based your faith, prayer life, and thinking?

Day 30

> Now to Him who is able to do immeasurably more than all we ask or imagine, according to His power that is at work within us … (Ephesians 3:20)

This is your reality: God's power is available to you. He *lives* in you! And because of His great love and mercy for you, you can truly depend on Him to do all that He promises! In response to this truth, proclaim the nine battle cries you have been introduced to. Please, *say them out loud* so your words will land on your ears and encourage your heart and mind!

1. My life of prayer produces peace and right thinking!
2. I trust my faithful God no matter what I see or feel!
3. I am the King's daughter; confidence and courage belong to me!
4. My eyes are fixed on the cross. I overcome through Christ's forgiveness and resurrection!
5. I walk in the confidence of Jesus Christ's love and mercy!
6. I forgive others and release them to Christ. I receive His abundant healing!
7. Out of a grateful heart, I walk in obedience, relying on God and the power of His love!
8. I submit to the sanctification process of the Holy Spirit!
9. I surrender to God's Word and Spirit. Holiness and humility are my standard!

Obedience

Creating Your Own Battle Cry

Now it's your turn. It is time for you to create and proclaim your personal battle cry. You may wish to create one battle cry or several. Create as many as you need to walk in freedom and be effective in God's kingdom! Our prayer is that you will use your battle cry as a warrior uses her sword. Your personal battle cry is a weapon in your arsenal, ready for action. Use it daily to refocus your mind on the truth. Use it when your heart is weak and you need your faith invigorated. Use it as a guidepost to keep you on the path with Jesus Christ. Memorize it; master it through regular use; and overcome with it!

Your Personal Battle Cry

Your battle cry will be built on truth; it will be designed to inspire you into greater belief through intentional thinking. Now create your custom battle cry, relevant to *your* life. Write it in present tense, as what you *are* doing, not what you want to do or will do, but what you are doing from this day forward. It is important that your battle cry is powerful and meaningful to you. Here are some questions to help you create your personal battle cry:

Day 30

- Has something you've read in this devotional struck a chord within you as an area in which you need victory?

- Have you thought about what ideas or words you will include in your battle cry?

- In what areas did you experience freedom by utilizing the three keys to intentional thinking?

- What have you determined to be your biggest struggle? Is it perhaps forgiveness, anger, fear, an addiction or unhealthy dependency, or an issue of sin?

Day 30

- What would your life be like if you overcame these struggles?

- How would your attitude and prayer life be impacted by overcoming?

Obedience

- How will you overcome? Will you fight? Stand? Kneel? Charge? Pray? Speak? Surrender? Believe? Contend?

My Battle Cry!

Day 30

Call to Action

Daughter of the Most High King, you are a warrior armed for victory! Fight the good fight. Never relent in doing good. Take up your call to impact the kingdom of God. Prayer is the catalyst for your victory. Write out your warrior prayer here.

Your Warrior Prayer

About the Authors

Sherry Rose, DTh

Sherry Rose has a heart to see God's kingdom operating in fullness through unity within the body of Christ. She is passionate about enriching life and fulfilling destiny. She pursues every opportunity to minister the restorative Word and ever-powerful love of God. Sherry has a bachelor of arts degree in psychology, a master of theology degree in Christian counseling, and a doctorate in theology with a leadership focus.

Sherry has studied domestic violence impact and recovery and is trained in grief and trauma counseling. She also has many years of experience in church-based women's ministry; specific-issue, small-group counseling; and personal development. In her role as a public speaker and Bible teacher, she exhorts women in the topics of courage, embracing the unexpected, living life fully with God's grace, personal identity and discovery, destiny, and now, intentional thinking!

In 2010, the Lord birthed a vision for a nonprofit ministry that He called Wellspring and based on Isaiah 58:11. In 2011 Sherry founded Wellspring Kingdom

Enrichment, a 501(c)(3) nonprofit organization in Bakersfield, California. She is the organization's president. Visit the website at www.wellspring-journey.com. Feel free to e-mail Sherry at sherry_wellspring@yahoo.com.

Jennifer Morin, MTh

Jennifer Morin's foremost passion is to motivate Christians to fully abide in the Lord and submit to the counsel and conviction of the Holy Spirit. She desires to see the children of God daily experience the presence of God. Jennifer received a bachelor's degree in 2000 as well as a master's degree in Christian counseling and leadership in 2013. Her multifaceted ministry involvement has given her experience in church administration, event planning, teaching, and prayer teams, as well as youth and women's ministry. She also organizes outreaches to the impoverished communities in her hometown.

In 2013, Jennifer formed Discipleship House Ministries as a resource to the community of wounded Christians. Her desire to see the body of Christ healthy led her to form this 501(c)(3) nonprofit organization to serve as a refuge for those who have been hurt by the church. Too often the pain of a church-hurt interferes with the wounded Christian's relationship with God. She formed this ministry to restore the disenchanted and wounded to fellowship with God. Jennifer encourages, counsels, and prays the hurting, helping them through to healing and hope, back into the fullness of God's presence.

Her goal in speaking, teaching, counseling, and coaching is to inspire each person to hunger after God and abide in Him daily. This results in Spirit-led living and freedom (John 15). Since earning her master's degree in Christian counseling, Jennifer's mission has been to assist the body of Christ in overcoming strongholds and sinful behaviors that stifle believers' spiritual growth. Jennifer makes herself available to those who truly want to discover the power of using their authority in Christ and the gifts of the Holy Spirit to find the freedom and abundance Jesus provides!

Her family lives and serves in Central California. She ministers, speaks, and serves where doors open and the Lord leads. E-mail her at mrsjennifermorin@gmail.com.

Printed in the United States
By Bookmasters